MARGATE CITY PUBLIC LIBRARY

8100 ATLANTIC AVENUE

MARGATE CITY, NJ 08402

(609) 822-4700

www.margatelibrary.org

1. Most items may be checked out for two weeks and renewed for the same period. Additional restrictions may apply to high-demand items.

2. A fine is charged for each day material is not returned according to the above rule. No material will be issued to any person incurring such a fine until it has been paid.

3. All damage to material beyond reasonable wear and all losses shall be paid for.

4. Each borrower is responsible for all items checked out on his/her library card and for all fines accruing on the same.

DEC   2011

DEMCO

SILVER
LIKE
DUST

SILVER
LIKE
DUST

*One Family's Story of
America's Japanese Internment*

KIMI CUNNINGHAM GRANT

PEGASUS BOOKS
NEW YORK

SILVER LIKE DUST
Pegasus Books LLC
80 Broad Street, 5th Floor
New York, NY 10004

Copyright © 2011 Kimi Cunningham Grant

First Pegasus Books January 2012

Interior design by Maria Fernandez

Library of Congress Cataloging-in-Publication Data is available.

ISBN: 978-1-60598-272-4

10 9 8 7 6 5 4 3 2 1

Printed in the United States of America
Distributed by W. W. Norton & Company

for my grandmothers

SILVER
LIKE
DUST

Prologue

FOR SO MANY YEARS, SHE WAS A MYSTERY TO ME: A shadow slipping among bodies; a set of hands; a background fixture, dim and indistinct. Sometimes, she read, seated upright on the white couch of her living room, her chin tucked, her lips faintly moving as her eyes swept across the page. But mostly she worked, leaning over steaming pots, her glasses fogged, her dark skin sticky with steam, or yanking weeds from among the hibiscus and azalea in the courtyard, or snapping peas at the kitchen table.

When my brother and I visited, she didn't swoop us up in an embrace the minute we arrived and stepped out of the car and onto the hot Florida pavement. She didn't gush over how much I'd grown, or hold me out at arm's length, studying my face, searching for changes, the way my grandfather, my Ojichan, did. She didn't play with us the way he did either. My grandfather would purchase masks for our visit, then hide and jump out to scare us. Our shrill screams would echo through the house, and we'd run away in delight. He gave us piggyback rides and romped around the living room. Obaachan, however, kept her distance, glancing up from her book as we raced by.

If she called our house in Pennsylvania, whether in October for my mother's birthday, or on Christmas afternoons, I would know her by her request to speak to my mother, and by her accent, the intonation imposed from another language, the strange rise and fall of the syllables. But I didn't recognize her voice.

We were at her house in Florida, standing in the hallway just inside the front door, when my mother first told me that my grandparents had spent nearly three years in a concentration camp. I was eight or nine years old. It was summertime, oppressively hot and humid, and we were there for our annual visit. In the living room, my grandfather was chasing my brother around the couch, and in the kitchen, my grandmother was washing dishes. With furtive glances toward her parents, my mother hissed this information, softly, like a confession. Or maybe it was more like an apology. I didn't ask any questions upon hearing this news, I think because I was afraid. Afraid of the way my mother's dark eyes looked at me solemnly, as though she were entrusting me with some grave secret. Or perhaps I was afraid of the answer, of the weight that the *why* behind this revelation might bring to my small shoulders. Whatever my reasons, all I knew at the time was that my Obaachan and Ojichan had been imprisoned for being Japanese, and I concluded from this conversation that there was something inherently bad about being Japanese, that there was something to be sorry about.

Had my parents chosen to raise their family in Hawaii, or California, where there are many people of Asian ancestry, or even in some urban area with general ethnic diversity, I might have been more likely to embrace my Japanese heritage as an adolescent. But they chose a small town in Pennsylvania, my white father's home, nestled in the farmed and mined folds of the state's midsection. My brother and I were two of a handful of minorities in our entire school district. It was not an ideal place for me to sort out issues of racial identity. I spent much of my young life trying to fit in, to be like everyone else around me—and to seem as un-Japanese as possible. I resisted my grandfather's attempts to teach me his language, squirmed in the dining-room chair and told him I couldn't do it, that the characters were too difficult, that I couldn't spit out the sounds. I resented, summer after summer, the Japanese exchange students my mother invited to our home and expected me to haul along on outings with friends. I turned up my nose at her puffy white *mochi* and pretended to gag on her *sushi*. "We don't like this stuff," I told her, dragging my brother into the declaration. "We're *American*."

Of course, I was oblivious to the fact that in all my efforts to be un-Japanese, I was joining that same old—and very Japanese—narrative of *haji*, or shame, that my mother had been participating in when she'd whispered her secret about my grandparents. The same one that had kept my family silent about those years in a Wyoming prison camp.

It was not until a decade after learning that Obaachan and Ojichan had lived at Heart Mountain that I began to pursue the answers to those questions that had lain dormant since my mother's confession. Despite my family's reticence regarding this portion of their history, I hoped my grandmother, that mysterious woman from my childhood, might be convinced to talk about it. That we hardly knew each other seemed only a minor hindrance: I was, after all, her granddaughter, and her namesake, and it had been more than sixty years since this all happened. My grandfather had passed away when I was a teenager, so Obaachan was alone now, and perhaps interested in a visitor. I called her, asked, with just a little bit of anxiety, whether I could visit, and when she said yes, I bought a plane ticket to Florida. I planned to spend a week with her at her home in Melbourne, on the Atlantic coast.

Convincing Obaachan, however, to resurrect her memories, to sift through them, blow off the dust, give them to me, and most significant of all, to let me write them down, was not the simple process I had naïvely anticipated. While I recognized immediately on that first trip to Melbourne that Obaachan was indeed glad to see me—that she was thrilled to have a week with her granddaughter—I also discovered quickly that she would rather talk about Elizabeth Bennet or Jane Eyre or Howard Roark than about herself. During the war, she learned to immerse herself in their stories, when reading was the only escape from that barren patch of Wyoming. Knowing there were hundreds of tales—of worlds—that she could flee to when the war stretched on and leaving Heart Mountain seemed itself a fiction, kept her going. Now that her children were grown and she had fewer obligations, she made weekly visits to the local library, checked book reviews, and read hundreds of pages a month.

Still, despite her affection for stories, my grandmother resisted telling her own, and she was especially hesitant to allow me to retell it. Opening up to others was not a comfortable act for her. There was the obvious issue of privacy. My grandmother, like most Japanese her age, valued her space and her right to keep to herself.

There were things a person didn't talk about, topics that were simply not meant for public eyes and ears. You turned your head when someone was changing clothes. You didn't meddle in a neighbor's failing marriage. You didn't pry.

More significant than the matter of privacy, however, was the issue of *haji*. Even six decades after World War II, my grandmother still felt shame about what had happened. She still experienced a pang of humiliation when she thought about Pearl Harbor, the thousands who were killed on that fateful Sunday morning, and when she recalled the early months of 1942, when *hakujin* journalists fabricated rumors in American newspapers and called the Japanese "vipers" and other names. She still shuddered when she remembered the long walk from Heart Mountain's changing room to the shower, naked. I quickly realized that shame, central to Japanese culture, was not a sentiment that sixty years could dissolve.

And so at first, getting my grandmother to talk was much like a negotiation, or a game. I might even compare our early conversations to the Japanese game of Go—the game that keeps old men staring for hours at a checkerboard of squares, cautiously maneuvering their smooth black and white stones. A game of psychology and power. Of conquering territory. Obaachan sat at her dining-room table in Melbourne, the Florida sun seeping in through the window and settling on her hands. She looked intently at the blue-and-white tablecloth, with its orderly shapes and lines, and began sliding her left thumb back and forth across the right one. The sun flickered from one hand to the other. Her lips twisted from side to side, and she frowned.

"Why don't you make it fiction?" she said at last, looking up at me and offering a sanguine little smile. "I could give you some information, and you could imagine the rest of it. You know, make it up."

Fiction would be easier. From the pieces of information I'd gathered already, I felt convinced I could weave quite a story. I knew, for instance, that my grandmother was one of 112,000 Japanese Americans who were displaced during the war. I knew that she was twenty years old when she was torn from her home in Los Angeles and shipped off to prison, and that she spent four months living in a barn at the Pomona Fairgrounds while the permanent camp in Wyoming was being finished. And I knew it was in prison that she met and married my grandfather, and gave birth to her first child, my uncle Charles. I knew, also, that after two years in that dusty Wyoming prison, she was desperate to leave, and did, when the opportunity came, but in doing so, missed the final days of her mother's life—something she still seemed to feel guilty about. The components were there: the narrative tension, the conflict, the compelling characters. I could dream up the rest.

The problem was, I didn't want to dream it up. I didn't want to speculate and concoct. Instead, I wanted to hear that "true" story in my grandmother's words, from her mouth. I wanted to see the way she told it: the way her fingers flexed or fiddled with something as she remembered an event, the way her eyes brightened or looked down. And there was more. In all of my recollections of childhood, my grandfather, Ojichan, stood in the forefront, looming, commanding, telling stories of his own. Obaachan stood behind him, in silence. I wanted to give a voice to this woman, a person forced into quiet by the noise of those around her. Writing her story seemed a way to do that.

But writing someone's story—especially the story of a loved one—is a task fraught with complexity. For starters, I recognized that the mere elasticity of language would not allow me to tell my grandmother's story as it truly was, or is. It would, necessarily, be a reconstruction, infused with my own literary preferences and my own writerly tics. Also, while I was committed to telling Obaachan's story as she told it to me, I knew that what she told me was itself shaped by decades of life that not only hindered the recollection of what had happened, but likely altered it as well. The space of sixty years takes its toll on the memory; like water, it smoothes and erodes and modifies the original shapes of things. Events jumble their order and grow hazy. Another person's memories blend with your own. Names, colors, buildings, faces, the everyday smells and tastes are elusive, if not altogether absent. In the case of my grandmother, remembering proved particularly complicated. She had devoted sixty years to trying to forget—to shuffling the painful past to a corner of her mind where she couldn't feel it, where it didn't haunt her.

I realized, too, that my grandmother was only giving me part of the story. Her account was of course subjective—her mother, father, and my grandfather would all have their own versions of things—but in addition to that, Obaachan would intentionally leave things out, especially details that might seem uncomplimentary to my grandfather, or her siblings. In the end, I was really only reconstructing her reconstruction: I was working only with the details she could, or would, give me. And yet a reconstruction felt more authentic than a fictionalization.

I told her I felt strongly about trying to write her life as it really was.

Obaachan shrugged her shoulders at this, and held out her hands, palms up, empty. "But my life has been very boring, you see. I'm sure nobody wants to know about it."

I explained to her then that in high school, in my American history textbook, there was a small, half-page box on the left-hand side of the page that covered the internment camps the US government had built for the Japanese they forced out of the West Coast. In class we fluttered past that box and marched through the rest of World War II. We absolutely discussed the December 7 bombing of Pearl Harbor, and we definitely spent some time going over Roosevelt's declaration of war, and most certainly we devoted some hours to Hitler and his camps. But we didn't talk about *our* camps.

"Some people don't even know it happened," I said, pausing, looking at her. "And they should know," I added, hoping that her sense of justice might convince her to speak, to say the difficult *yes*.

Still hesitant, she took a sip of coffee and then placed her mug carefully on the table. "Well," she said after a few moments, frowning a little bit, "if we do this, you can't use my real name. Or anyone else's either. I don't want people to be able to figure out it's me."

I nodded. Part of me worried that we were blurring that already messy line separating nonfiction from fiction, but at that point, names seemed a minor detail.

"I mean, everyone's still alive. Except your Ojichan. And my parents. But my brothers and my sister, my children, they're living. So you'll have to keep them out of it. You can't tell their stories. It's not my place to do that, to speak for them. It's not right."

I attempted, graciously, I hoped, to change her mind. "We can't tell your story without telling at least a little bit of theirs," I said. "People will want to know that both of your brothers served in the US military, that they stayed faithful in their commitment to the country, even when you and your parents were living as prisoners. They'll wonder where your sister and her family ended up, because they'll know that she wasn't with you in Wyoming. People will want to know," I told her. "And the story won't work if there are too many holes." At last we agreed on creating pseudonyms based on their initials, and we settled on sharing just a little bit—just enough to keep the story cohesive— about the siblings. The same rules would apply to my aunts and uncles as well.

Finally, after a good deal of this negotiating back and forth, my grandmother agreed. Year by year, memory by memory, as each one swam back to her, she passed them on to me. Her recollections were rarely in order, and on occasion we ended up looping back to rethink incongruent details. Together, we began the slow, cautious dance of reconstructing 1941 through 1945, the years that so profoundly shaped four generations of my family, years we had all tried to forget.

Chapter 1

OBAACHAN FILLS THE THERMOS WITH COFFEE AND THEN we head to the beach to have breakfast and see the sunrise, to watch it color the water gold as it spills over the Atlantic. At this hour, all of Melbourne's banks and strip malls are still closed, and only a handful of cars sit in their parking lots. We drive over the wide Indian River, and I focus my eyes ahead, at the grass and trees, instead of peering out at the water's peaks and ripples. I've inherited my mother's unfortunate fear of bridges, and my palms grow clammy at the wheel as we cross the river. At last, we reach land, wait at a few stoplights, and pull into a public parking lot along the shore. It's overcast, and so there is no brilliant sunrise; there is only a long, deserted beach and burning wind and a wide, restless stretch of sea. Thermos and plastic bag in hand, we make our way to a worn wooden observation deck and settle on a bench. We take out the strawberry cobbler we made earlier in the week, which is soggy and too sweet, and which we've been eating incessantly, it seems, for three days now. My grandmother, clearly a product of the Great Depression, refuses to throw it away, even though she admits it's no good.

"Well, what exactly do you want to know?" she says slowly, opening the thermos and pouring herself a cup of steaming coffee. She replaces the lid and then turns to look out at the water. This bewildering straightforwardness, I am learning during my week with my grandmother, is one of her distinct characteristics, and it still catches me by surprise. She will keep quiet; she will not often press for details or demand that things go her way. She is perfectly content to listen without offering any advice. Yet at the same time, she seems to disapprove of tiptoeing around difficult issues once they present themselves. She believes in being direct, especially when she is ready to be direct.

Still, after three days of carefully probing and hinting at my desire to know about her past, I'm somehow unprepared for this sudden willingness to talk. Part of the problem is that I want to know everything. The sting of reading the signs that hung from storefronts and warned, in all capital letters, "JAPS KEEP OUT, YOU RATS!" The ingredients of the final meal the family shared before they left their home forever. The process of deciding which items to take with her, which possessions were important enough to carry all that way—or rather, which ones she could bear to leave behind. I want to know how she felt at this moment, and what she thought at another moment, and what she wore and heard and said and smelled and tasted. But we must begin somewhere, this mining of the memory, and now, after so much pleading for her to tell the story, I don't really know where to start.

Obaachan takes a bite of the strawberry cobbler and then places her plastic fork on a napkin beside her. Perhaps she senses the reasons behind my silence, or knows that I'm not sure what to say. Or perhaps it is sitting on the beach that stirs her, because as she looks out at the gray Atlantic, a memory comes to her, and with a hint of a smile, she begins. "When the four of us were young," she says, hesitating, "we spent Sunday afternoons at the beach."

Their beach, that is: the only one they were allowed on, Brighton Beach. They weren't permitted to go to Venice Beach, or to Santa Monica Beach or to any of the other beaches in Los Angeles. Those were *hakujin* beaches. Whites-only beaches.

Obaachan's Mama spent Saturday evenings preparing for the Sunday outing. She fried chicken in *teriyaki* sauce, and the strong scent of *shoyu* filled the house. She steamed rice and rolled it into tidy little spheres. She cut up cucumbers or some other fresh vegetable, and sometimes, on special occasions, she sliced watermelon. And then she packed all of it into her set of stackable square containers. They ate lunch right after arriving, and then they would swim or build sandcastles or play paddleball.

When night fell, Papa dug a pit and started a fire, and the family gathered around. The boys, Ren and Jack, found six sticks and shaved off the bark, then gave one to each person. Mama and Sachiko, Obaachan's older sister, unpacked the hot dogs they'd brought, and over the flames the meat would sizzle and spit. Papa told stories and the waves tumbled and snarled at their backs, and the salt dried in sinuous paths on their skin, and right there, in the balmy glow of the fire, Papa's face fell into a thousand lines of laughter.

This was long before the war, in the thirties. Long before Mama got sick and long before they lost everything and were forced out of Los Angeles. They were happy, the six of them. Never rich, but never hungry or in need. In that sense, they were better off than a lot of people during the Depression. Papa's job, at least to a degree, could be credited for this. He worked as a traffic director at a produce market and could bring home fresh vegetables and fruit each day.

Obaachan's mother simply planned the family's meals around whatever he provided. At the market, farmers would drive their pickup trucks loaded with bushels of vegetables and fruit to the market and sell them to various vendors, who would then take the produce to grocery stores. Papa worked odd hours, getting up and leaving before three o'clock in the morning and working until lunchtime. He did this six days a week. Usually, he would use those precious hours while the children were still at school to sleep, and then he would spend evenings with the family.

Papa had come to America around 1910, and Mama, a "picture bride" whose parents had arranged the marriage back in Japan, arrived a few years later. Both of them were from Wakayama, a rural province known for its hot springs and temples. They wed in December of 1915, and eventually they saved up enough money to buy a house on a double lot in Los Angeles. They were from Japan, so they could not become citizens. The Naturalization Act of 1790 limited naturalized citizenship to "free whites," and although in 1868 the Fourteenth Amendment extended this to African Americans, it was not until 1954 that Asian immigrants could become naturalized citizens. California's 1913 Alien Land Law prohibited noncitizens from owning land, but Papa and Mama, like many Japanese families, sidestepped the stipulations of this law by deeding the house in the names of their children, who had been born in the United States and were therefore rightful citizens.

The house on Pico Street, a small frame house with a large covered front porch, sat on the back half of the lot. Papa transformed the front half of it into a botanical oasis, a haven in the midst of so much pavement. He poured himself into that garden, planting and watering, weeding and pruning. At the time of the evacuation, he had over thirty varieties of plants. Bamboo, camellias, wisteria, oleanders—all of them were, like so many other pieces of their life, left behind.

Obaachan shrugs, wrapping her fingers around the metal cup from the thermos and resting it on her knees. She takes a deep breath. "*Hakabanohana* is the name for oleander in Japanese. *Hakabano* means 'burial ground' and *hana* means 'flower.' So the actual word means 'burial flower.' Most Japanese consider them bad luck. But Papa liked them and planted them anyway." She smiles a little. "We were only superstitious sometimes."

In one of my grandmother's photographs, her father is standing in his garden, in front of a forsythia heavy with blossoms. He is wearing a dark three-piece suit, and he is holding his fedora hat suspended above his head, as though greeting the person taking the picture. It's not an ostentatious gesture; it's more one of deference. Although he does not smile, his mouth is turned slightly upward, and his eyes are tranquil and kind. Even the black-and-white image captures a distinct air of dignity and composure. It is the only picture Obaachan has of her father in middle age, as she would have known him.

"We used to catch bees," she says, kicking her legs back and forth. On the wooden bench, her feet do not touch the ground. She watches a pair of gulls swing toward the water. "There were always so many of them, buzzing and swirling in the garden, and we'd wait with our glass jars and then scoop them right in, like this." She imitates the motion. "And fireflies, too."

She tells me that one of their neighbors, the tall man with strong black arms, grew tomato plants once, and that when he showed them to her from across the fence, she couldn't believe those full red fruits could grow on such spindly limbs. And that one year, Papa let her till up a spot of his garden to grow sweet corn. That her mouth watered every day when she inspected the tall plants, waiting for them to be ready, and that Papa had to tell her again and again, *wait*. From the way she talks about him, I can tell that Obaachan respected her father immensely, that she recalls him as fearless, strong, and wise. In another one of her photographs, Papa is seated beside his own father, and he stares indifferently, somberly, outward. And in a third photograph, Papa has the same serious expression, only in that one, he is standing beside his new wife, who looks equally somber. They have probably just met.

"My father only had an eighth-grade education," Obaachan says, pulling her navy cardigan more tightly over her shoulders as the wind picks up, "but he knew so much. He could fix almost anything, and, well, he just seemed to understand how things worked."

Like many *Issei*, or first-generation, men, Papa had initially found work in America as a gardener for the wealthy. Before he was hired to direct trucks at the produce place, he simply walked from door to door, knocking and asking owners if they were in need of someone to help with the gardening. Many *hakujin* were interested in hiring Japanese gardeners, for people quickly realized that most of them were knowledgeable, hardworking, good with the land, and, most importantly, that their labor could be had at a low price. In fact, it did not take long for the Japanese to develop quite a reputation all along the West Coast for being capable farmers.

Their success with the land, however, came at a cost: many of their *hakujin* neighbors began to begrudge these accomplishments, and eventually, this bitterness blossomed into a general dislike of the Japanese as a race. In a March 9, 1905, article titled "The Yellow Peril: How the Japanese Crowd out the White Race," one San Francisco *Chronicle* journalist wrote:

The market gardening industry has to some extent been occupied by the Chinese, but in the main it has been held by white men, mostly Europeans . . . In some places this is rapidly passing to the Japanese, because their living expenses are nominal. With no idle mouths to feed they herd in old shacks, and can exist and lay up money where any white man will starve . . .

It took very little time for such sour resentment to surface and, looking back at the history of Asians in the United States, it makes sense that the hostility with which the Japanese were received was merely a continuation of the anti-Asian sentiments that had existed for years. After all, the Japanese were not the first to experience such antipathy. The Chinese had come to America decades earlier, during the 1849 gold rush. Then, in the 1860s, more of them had followed, knowing they could find employment in the construction of the transcontinental railroad. Working at much cheaper rates than their white counterparts, the Chinese were viewed with antagonism. They were stealing jobs from white men. They "work[ed] cheap and smell[ed] bad" and were subhuman, as Professor Elmer Sandmeyer, attempting to describe how white Americans perceived Chinese immigrants, wrote in his 1939 study titled *The Anti-Chinese Movement in California*. They were—as the 1879 California

Constitution itself stated—"dangerous and detrimental to the well-being or peace of the state."

This hostile mind-set toward the Chinese transferred easily to the Japanese. In 1884, after centuries of strictly closed borders, the emperor of Japan finally began allowing emigration to the United States, and the Japanese came to America quickly, in great sweeps. By 1892, only a couple thousand Japanese had settled on the mainland, but Californian Denis Kearney, leader of the Workingman's Party, ended a speech with this statement: "The Japs must go!" While Kearney's call resonated with many Californians, it did little to curb immigration. Despite their poor reception, the Japanese continued pouring into California. By 1900, there were around twenty-five thousand Japanese living on the West Coast. That year, J. D. Phelan, the mayor of San Francisco, claimed, "The Chinese and Japanese are not bona fide citizens. They are not the stuff of which American citizens can be made . . ."

Obaachan folds her hands and places them in her lap. "We certainly had our own separate spaces," she says quietly. On the beach below, a jogger passes and nods to us in greeting. Obaachan slides a finger along the edge of the bench, tracing the grain of the wood. "At the movie theatres, there were two levels: the first floor, and a balcony. Mama used to take us to matinees, before she got sick. I don't know if it was a law or if the studios just had a policy, but I know that I was always seated in the balcony, with the blacks and Mexicans, and other Japanese and Chinese, and that I never once sat on the first floor. Only the *hakujin* sat down there."

There were similar rules with other public areas. The roller-skating rink was only open to Japanese on Sunday nights; they could not go any other day of the week. They were only permitted to use public tennis courts on Sundays as well. And they were not allowed to swim in public pools. "I remember that the *Rafu Shimpo*, the Japanese newspaper in LA, would have a large sports section on Mondays," Obaachan says. "Only one day of the week because all the Japanese sporting events were held on Sundays. It was the only day we were allowed to use public areas for things like tennis." She pauses, frowning, tapping her index finger on the wooden bench. "And we mostly shopped in Little Tokyo, or at very large department stores. We didn't go in the smaller *hakujin* stores."

As I listen to my grandmother talk, I cannot help noticing the contradiction—the odd and complicated problem of *what preceded what.* Japanese immigrants were not legally allowed to become citizens. They were not hired by white employers. They were not permitted to integrate in social spheres. And yet they were criticized by the public and the media for just that: for not fitting in, for keeping to themselves, for not being "bona fide citizens," for not being *American*.

Perhaps not surprisingly, both the government and the media played a role in developing the notion of "the yellow peril." In 1901, the United States Industrial Commission released a statement claiming that the Japanese were ". . . as a class tricky, unreliable, and dishonest." The San Francisco *Chronicle*, arguably the most influential newspaper on the West Coast at the time, began a lengthy anti-Japanese campaign in February of 1903, seven years before my grandmother's family had arrived in America. The campaign opened with this front-page streamer: "The Japanese Invasion, The Problem of the Hour." The paper asserted that Japanese men were a danger to American women, and claimed that "every one of these immigrants . . . is a Japanese spy."

Obaachan looks at me, squinting a little as the wind blows more violently. Grains of sand tumble across the boardwalk, hissing against the wood. "But, you see, Mama and Papa worked very hard to instill a positive attitude in us children," she says. "No matter what happened." You didn't complain about unfairness or inequality. You didn't resent the hurtful or negative things that happened to you. You followed the rules. You didn't resist. "There's a word for it," Obaachan says, "*shikataganai.*"

There are things that cannot be changed, and you don't try to change them.

Shikataganai is a new word to me, and I wonder if it's a word I will ever really understand. It lurches off the tongue in spasms of hard sounds: *k, t, g.* Its very notion feels un-American, that some things are unchanging, or unchangeable. I am too much of an optimist—or maybe just too much a product of the late-twentieth century—to accept this word the way my grandmother does. I consider all of this, frown, and take a sip of coffee.

"It's a way of thinking," Obaachan explains, watching me. She leans forward and crosses her legs at the ankles, her Easy Spirit tennis shoes clean and bright in the early morning gray. "It's a saying that all Japanese told each other when something unfair was happening, like the laws, or the headlines that said everyone was a spy or that we were all sneaks. Even in the concentration camp, people would shrug their shoulders and say, '*Shikataganai.*'" She searches my face and senses that I don't grasp it, that I fail to understand how a group of people could collectively embrace such an attitude. "You don't get it because you were born so much later," she says. "You have to remember, this was before the civil rights movement. We didn't even know about rights. It wasn't in our vocabulary. Everything was very different."

Just five years before Obaachan's father arrived, in 1905, the Asiatic Exclusion League was established, with the primary goal of halting immigration from Japan and even expelling the Japanese already established in California. The league, along with groups like the American Legion, the Native Sons of the Golden West, and the State Federation of Labor, pushed for a 1920 version of the Alien Land Law, which would prohibit the Japanese from accessing farmland altogether, whether by buying it or leasing it, regardless of whether or not they were citizens. Finally, under the provisions of the 1924 Immigration Act, it became illegal for people ineligible for citizenship—which meant, essentially, those of Asian descent—to immigrate at all to the United States. By that time, Obaachan's parents had already settled on Pico Street and started their family.

A significant turning point in the movement to exclude the Japanese occurred on October 11, 1906, when the San Francisco School Board ordered all Japanese children to attend the segregated Oriental School, where Chinese children were required to go. Although this action went largely unnoticed in the United States, the Japanese press—and Japan—was outraged. The act violated a clause from the 1894 Commerce and Navigation treaty the two countries had signed, and the Japanese knew it. So did Theodore Roosevelt. He called the action "intemperate" and deemed Californians "idiots" for instigating an international conflict that reached far beyond the city limits of San Francisco. In an attempt to resolve the problem, Roosevelt, in what became known as the "Gentlemen's Agreement," eventually did the following: he convinced the school board to reinstate the Japanese students into their original schools; put an end to Japanese immigration to Mexico, Canada, and Hawaii; and persuaded the Japanese government to stop issuing passports to laborers. The Gentlemen's Agreement, then, achieved precisely what the exclusionists had been pushing for: it slowed down the tide of immigration.

"I know you have trouble understanding," Obaachan says slowly, "but it never occurred to me to feel upset about the way the *hakujin* thought of us, or to complain about how we were treated." She pauses, fiddling with a button on her sweater. "We understood that we were not part of their world."

Obaachan turns toward the ocean and watches the water froth and sputter as it crashes below. Far away, where the water meets the sky, a boat passes. "Besides," she says softly, "we had our own family struggles to worry about. Things that seemed more pressing. My spinal meningitis. I was just a small girl when I got it. Seven, maybe eight years old."

She was quarantined at the hospital, unable to see her parents or siblings, and she vividly remembers the morning when the doctor and nurses came in to draw spinal fluid with a long needle. "They thought I might die," she whispers. But, after a few days, she was sent home and told to stay in bed for a week. Everything seemed fine until one afternoon, when she picked up the telephone, held it to her left ear, and couldn't hear the voice on the other end. Because the hearing loss was only in one ear, she hadn't even realized what had happened.

"It's not a big deal, being deaf in one ear," she says with a shrug. "I just can't hear as well in a group of people, like when the whole family gets together, or when someone talks very quietly. If they're sitting on the wrong side, it's hard for me to hear what they're saying."

I can't help but wonder if my grandmother's quietness all these years might stem, at least in part, from this hearing issue. Combined with her shyness and my grandfather's spirited and garrulous nature, it's no wonder Obaachan rarely joined a conversation.

"More than my own sickness, though," she continues, "was my mother's illness. That was much more, well, much more of an upset to our family life."

Obaachan had just turned thirteen when her mother learned she had an irregular heartbeat. With the diagnosis, Mama essentially became an invalid and was confined to her bed. Up to that point, she had been an active mother, playing with the children, taking them to matinees and the city library, cooking, cleaning, and attending to all the household duties. When she was warned by her doctors that she needed to limit her activities to avoid straining her weak heart, however, all of this came to an end. There were no more family outings on Sunday afternoons or after school, and the daughters had to take over Mama's chores at the house.

For Obaachan's sister, the transition was not that momentous. Sachiko was five years older, and, at eighteen, had finished high school. She'd already negotiated those difficult years when the body stretches and swells, when new colors drop from it, when new aches weigh it down. Sachiko spent her days working as a cashier at a nearby Japanese grocery store and devoted her evenings to sewing. Bent over at the kitchen table, straining and concentrating beneath the tepid glow of the overhead light, she measured and cut, pinned and then stitched together the fabrics. She was making herself a new wardrobe. She had a life, an existence that was about to extend itself beyond the small world of her parents.

For Obaachan, though, the changes brought on by Mama's illness were much more challenging. She was younger and more in need of maternal support. Every afternoon, right after school, she headed straight to her parents' bedroom, knocked on the door, and then entered when Mama called her in. She seated herself on the edge of the bed and talked about her day. Funny stories from math class. That a girl got in trouble for passing a note. How the social studies teacher, the one with lovely blonde hair, had married a World War I flying ace over the weekend, and how she had pasted his photograph on the bulletin board and told the class her last name was different now.

Mama was a good listener, but talking to her as she lay solemn and corpselike on her bed was not the same as it had once been. Before, Mama would listen to these stories from school, nodding and smiling, but also bustling about the kitchen, chopping a *daikon*, and then interrupting to ask for some fresh bamboo shoots from Papa's garden. The new Mama, the one who called out cooking instructions from her bed in a weak and raspy voice as the girls moved obediently about the kitchen, was different. Obaachan felt as though she were on the verge of losing something. The way it feels when you're caught between childhood and adulthood. When you wish for what is past but know you must move on.

Obaachan shakes her head sheepishly and then tells me that it was around this time that she decided to change her name.

"Not change it legally or anything," she adds, brushing her hands on her white cotton capris. "I made up a nickname. Or—what's the word?—a pseudonym of sorts."

I give her a confused look.

She smiles, a little mysterious, a little embarrassed. "Let me explain."

One of her hobbies was filling out forms for free samples. In magazines, or in line at the grocery store, there were forms for these from various companies that could be filled out and mailed in. "Cold cream, or a new shade of lipstick, or rouge. You just wrote your name and address on the little card, sent it in, and then, maybe nine or ten weeks later, you'd have a free sample in the mail." She didn't have money to spend on lipsticks or lotions. Nobody did. It was, she reminds me, the Great Depression.

"It was my friend Aiko who gave me the idea," Obaachan says. "She always entered contests to come up with jingles or taglines, and she told me that whenever she did that, she changed her name to sound Polish. And so one day, I just decided that I didn't want to use my real name when I requested the samples. So I filled in the same mailing address but listed my name as Grace Komak."

I ask her why she decided to do this, and it takes her a moment to answer. She picks up her mug, holds it out over the edge of the deck, and flicks her wrist to empty the remaining drops of coffee into the sand. She wraps a napkin around our plastic forks, which she will take home and reuse, and places them in the bag.

"My name sounded too Japanese," she says with a shrug, turning away from me, brushing off the question. But I sense from her guarded response that this decision was more momentous than she lets on, that somehow, though she won't admit it, there was *haji* in this act.

Chapter 2

EVERY NIGHT, OBAACHAN CHECKS THE LOCAL NEWS TO learn what time the sun will rise the next morning and then sets her alarm clock accordingly so that she can see it on her morning walk. The following day, my fourth in Florida, I hear her stirring, and I squint at the clock: 6:43 a.m. She calls to me from outside the closed bedroom door, and I tell her I'm up. I'd rather sleep for a few more hours, but there's something shameful about rolling out of bed after my octogenarian grandmother has already walked two miles, seen the sunrise, swept the courtyard, made breakfast, and read an editorial in *Time* magazine. Besides, if I want to get to know her better—and get her to tell more of her story—I've got to meet her on her terms. I force myself out of bed and get dressed.

Outside, the pavement is steaming from an overnight rain. Though it's barely seven o'clock, Obaachan's neighbors, mostly retirees, are up, walking for exercise, stooping at trees in their front yards and tugging at weeds, wheeling their trash down their driveways in giant beige garbage cans. I imagine some of them have been up for hours, sipping black coffee at their kitchen tables, waiting for dawn.

"Good morning, Elsa," Obaachan calls to the statuesque woman watering a hibiscus with giant red blossoms. The woman waves and saunters to the end of her driveway, her watering can resting against her hip. She says hello in a thick, throaty accent, then frowns, reaching out and squeezing my grandmother's hand. "I haven't seen you for a few days. I was worried. I'm glad you're all right." Elsa knows Obaachan lives alone at the end of the street, and that none of her children are nearby, and like a good neighbor, she keeps an eye on her. Elsa lets go of Obaachan and shifts to another subject. "Well, I saw on the news it's going to be hot today. That's why I'm out here early. I can't take the heat." She shakes her head and smiles. Elsa is tall and slender, and her hair is still a little bit blonde. I can tell that she was, in her younger years, quite attractive.

"How's Frank?" Obaachan asks.

Elsa sighs and shrugs her shoulders. She moves the watering can around as she speaks. "He's the same, I guess. Sometimes he remembers, sometimes not." She adjusts her white visor nervously and turns to me. "This must be your granddaughter," she says, as if she has suddenly realized I'm present. She moves in to shake my hand. Obaachan nods and offers an introduction. Elsa's fingers are lean and strong against mine. "Your grandmother has been talking about you for weeks."

I smile and make conversation, tell her I'm in my second year of college, that I'm majoring in English, that yes, I have a boyfriend named Chris, and that no, I don't know what I will do when I graduate. I say how lovely the weather is here in Florida, compared to Pennsylvania, where I've always lived. Elsa nods with interest, studying my face with her blue eyes, smiling at the word boyfriend. I wonder what my grandmother has told her about me in the preceding weeks, since, for most of my life, our relationship has consisted of seeing each other for a weeklong visit, once a year, and since the last time I saw her was when she came to visit over Christmas when I was a senior in high school. Our correspondence has been limited: she mails me birthday and Christmas cards, and I send her thank-you notes.

After a few minutes, Obaachan tells Elsa in her sweet, matter-of-fact way that we ought to be going, that we're exercising. When we've walked far enough past Elsa's house, Obaachan leans toward me and whispers, "Elsa's a war bride from Germany. Her husband, Frank, was stationed there when they met." We pass a small lake and a turtle scuttles in, disappearing.

"She often says snide remarks about Jewish people," Obaachan adds, smacking her lips and shaking her head in disapproval. "It's hard to believe, but after all these years, she still feels hate." After all these years. It occurs to me that here, in this slow, quiet neighborhood where every house is painted the same shadowy shade of peach, and where each perfect St. Augustine lawn stretches out in magnificent bright green, somebody might hate Obaachan, too. That somebody, perhaps the man who has floated past us on his bicycle, or maybe the gray-haired woman checking her mail, hasn't left the hatred from six decades ago behind. I think of all the headlines, posters, and pamphlets from the war, of the pictures I've been coming across in books, and I realize that just as Elsa has not been able to forget entirely the speeches and slogans from her childhood in Germany, there may be American neighbors here in Melbourne who hold on to those ideas from decades before.

In the two years prior to the bombing of Pearl Harbor, life on Pico Street began to change for Obaachan's family. In 1939 Obaachan's sister met and married a Japanese man. "He was so good-looking," Obaachan gushes, grinning. "He was one of the most handsome Japanese men I had ever met." She would have been eighteen at her sister's wedding, and her new brother-in-law would have been twenty-four. After the war, she saw him only a handful of times, and thus remembers him as a young man, so I suppose it's not surprising that her initial impression is so lasting, and that she remembers him with such girlish zeal.

"My sister moved out to live with her new husband," Obaachan says as we turn out of her neighborhood and cross the street. "A Japanese woman did not have many options back then. You could get married and have children. Or you might serve as a clerk, although only at a Japanese store—getting hired at a *hakujin* place was unheard of. And maybe, if you were really lucky, you might land a civil service job." She smiles, as if calculating how much has changed since then. "That was the most ambitious thing we would hope for: working for the civil service. You know, typing or doing accounting work."

Japanese families invested in their sons, and Obaachan's was no different. Although her sister, Sachiko, was the oldest, and perhaps the smartest and most driven, she was still a daughter, which meant that her parents would not spend money educating her. Ren was the second oldest, but the first son; his parents sent him to college. In May of 1941, he graduated from the University of Southern California as a pharmacist, passed the civil service exam, and got a job at Fresno Air Force Base. His parents had perhaps never been prouder. And then there was Obaachan, the demure middle child, and then Jack, the youngest, the little brother. He was the athlete, the family daredevil, the adventurous one.

"When I had a family of my own, I insisted that the daughters have all the same opportunities as the sons. That was one of the few things I put my foot down about with your grandfather," Obaachan explains. She slows her pace a little, looking at the ground. "I didn't want them to be like me."

What Obaachan does not tell me right then is that in the fall of 1941, she had applied, taken entrance exams, and been accepted at Los Angeles City College. She could attend for free, and since her parents would not have to fund her education, they supported the decision. They were happy to have her continue staying at home while she took classes. By that point she was the only one of their children who still lived with them, and at the time, her mother's care rested completely on her shoulders. Her father still worked long, odd hours at the produce market, and could only help at certain times, so Obaachan alone handled the cooking, cleaning, and shopping for her parents.

After graduating from high school, she had spent two years at home, not working but taking care of her ailing mother, and during that time she'd decided she wanted to go to college. She admits she was not sure what exactly she wanted to do with a college degree, but she recognized the link between choices and education. She knew she had little time before she'd be expected to marry and start a family, and at twenty, she wanted options. The opportunity to attend school for free seemed a remarkable blessing: it was her path out of living with her parents forever, being pushed into an arranged marriage, or working as a clerk in Little Tokyo for the rest of her life. Plus, because going to college had always been something so entirely out of reach for her, it was even more desirable. Obaachan started classes in January of 1942, but her goal of earning a college degree would never come to fruition. She didn't even finish a semester.

"We knew that a war was going on," Obaachan says, sliding her hands into the pockets of her cardigan. A runner, a woman in an all-pink Nike outfit, approaches on the walking path, and we switch to single file to allow her to pass. Obaachan continues. "I mean, my family listened to the reports on the radio. My Papa was the type of person who liked to stay informed. We knew that Japan had invaded China, and that it had formed an alliance with Germany and Italy. And we'd heard about the Nazis, how they had invaded Poland and Greece and Yugoslavia and many other places. It seemed like everyone was invading and bombing everyone else." She looks down and rubs at her knuckles. "But none of it had felt close. At least not for me."

Perhaps Obaachan's parents understood the events that were shaping the world in those years before Japan bombed Pearl Harbor better than she did. They had friends and family back in Japan and likely corresponded with them through letters, so they may have suspected that the war would eventually make its way to America. Obaachan herself remembers that in the thirties, a neighbor on Pico Street, a wild-eyed old man with fluffy white hair, predicted a war between the United States and Japan. Her parents, however, seemed unconcerned about their neighbor's ravings, nor did they express any anxiety about Japan's military decisions or the war in Europe. My grandmother, trained to follow her parents' moves and responses, shrugged off her old neighbor's prophecies—he was strange and slightly crazy, anyway—and thought little of the news reports on the radio each evening.

After all, for Obaachan, world geography would have been an altogether different concept than it had been for me. As a child, I leafed through color photographs in my parents' collection of *National Geographic* magazines and dreamed of traveling to exotic places when I grew up. I sensed, too, even as a kid, that doing so was within reach. For my grandmother, on the other hand, the European names and places she heard on her parents' shortwave radio were likely nothing more than words she had memorized in a high school history course. While she could identify the countries on a map, she knew nothing about them or their people. As a Japanese American living in the 1930s, she realized she wouldn't go to any of those places. They would never be anything but faraway locations, interesting for their architecture and sculptures, maybe, but nothing beyond that.

"I'd only left the United States one time, when my family went to Japan. I was very young," Obaachan says, and then she points out that we have reached the halfway point in our morning walk, exactly one mile, according to her calculations. We pause here. My grandmother has planned her walk perfectly. Just as we finish up this first leg of our trek, the sun peers over the horizon, lighting up the bright facades of stucco houses, casting long shadows across the grass. A light breeze lifts the fronds of a palm tree beside the path. We turn around and head back the way we came.

"I don't remember much about that trip to Japan," Obaachan continues. Her memories consist of scattered images. An endless float across the Pacific in a great gray ship. Having dinner at a restaurant in Wakayama. Meeting her mother's family, the quiet group of people she would never see again. Papa had stayed home to work and take care of the house, so it was only Mama and the four children who made the trip. "I was maybe seven years old. So you see," Obaachan explains, slowing her pace a little and using her hands for emphasis, "Japan was never home to me. It was only a place I had visited as a kid. Los Angeles was the only home I knew. I was born there. I was an American citizen. I was very aware that I was Japanese, of course, but I was a Japanese *American*. For us, there was a difference." But, as my grandmother was about to find out, for many Americans, there was no difference at all.

December 7, 1941, began much like every other Sunday for Obaachan's family. They woke up, had breakfast, and then walked to the morning service at the small Japanese Christian church near their home. When the service ended, they gathered with the rest of the congregation on the front steps to chat, just as they had done for years. Obaachan talked to some friends about heading to a matinee to see *The Maltese Falcon*, which had just premiered in October. And then, amid their laughter and planning—frantic shouts. A middle-aged man ran up the sidewalk, waving his arms and calling for attention. He slowed at the bottom of the steps, stopped to catch his breath, then panted out the news: Japan had bombed Pearl Harbor.

Panic erupted. Obaachan's family collected themselves and hurried home in a fog of confusion. They spent the afternoon huddled around the shortwave radio in the living room, listening to the accounts, sorting through the details, taking on the weight of what had happened. Papa sipped his black coffee and sat in his favorite chair, leaning forward, his elbows resting on his knees. Mama listened from her bed, lying on her side and watching her husband's face through the bedroom door. Obaachan stood in the corner of the room, taking it all in, her hands folded at her waist.

"Like I told you, none of it had felt close, at least not for me," Obaachan says softly. "I was only twenty, so maybe I was just uninformed or foolish. To me, all those names and places, the invasions—all of it was so far away."

And then suddenly, the war was there: trickling in through the radio, filling the house on Pico Street. Obaachan says she wasn't afraid that day, at least not for herself, or for her family, or for Japanese Americans. She understood that what had happened involved the two countries that most affected her, that composed her identity, but she did not consider the possibility that the United States' retaliation would also be aimed at the Japanese living on American soil. Mostly, she was shocked and sad. She imagined the thundering sounds of the bombs, the fiery chaos, the cries of terror. She shivered at the thought of so much destruction.

Obaachan may have been naïvely oblivious to what lay ahead for her and the other 110,000 people of Japanese descent living on the West Coast. (The West

Coast was eventually deemed a "military zone," which gave the government grounds for evacuation, but those Japanese who lived elsewhere in the United States were never removed from their homes.) Obaachan's father, however, may have had an intuition of what the future would hold. He said nothing at all about it that afternoon. Instead, he sat in grim silence, listening over and over to the reports on the radio, and it seemed that during the course of that day, he developed two tiny indentations on his forehead, one above each eyebrow, like the marks left by a hoe splitting the earth.

It turned out that the bombing of Pearl Harbor was only Japan's first step in a well-planned series of assaults. Within twenty-four hours, it launched attacks on Malaya, Hong Kong, Guam, the Philippines, Wake Island, and Midway Island. The morning after the initial bombing, President Roosevelt explained all of this in his "Day of Infamy" speech and declared war on Japan. In doing so, the United States entered World War II: three days later, the country was officially at war with Germany and Italy as well. On Monday, December 8, Obaachan's brother Ren went to work at his pharmacy and was asked, without explanation, to resign from his position at Fresno Air Force Base. In a single day, his schooling, testing, and hard work were stripped from him. No longer welcome on base, he returned to Los Angeles, and moved back into his parents' house. Two months later, he would be drafted into the US Army, and leave for basic training in Arkansas.

Obaachan's family chose not to view Ren's losing his job as an insult. They chose also to accept without bitterness the irony of his being drafted just a few months after Fresno had asked him to leave. Above all things, her family, like many Japanese Americans at the time, wished to demonstrate their patriotism to the United States. If it meant resigning from a job without a fuss, that's what should be done. If it meant being drafted and fighting in the American military, a person should be willing to go. When Ren was drafted, he had no way of knowing that his sisters and parents would soon be shipped off to spend the entirety of World War II behind barbed wire, but even if he had, my grandmother insists, he would have done the very same thing. Jack, Obaachan's younger brother, was also anxious to show his patriotism: shortly after Pearl Harbor was bombed, he enlisted in the US Army and eventually became a paratrooper.

I struggle to understand this painful sense of duty and devotion. Had it been my own brother who'd lost his hard-earned military job and then been forced to join a different branch of the military, I would have been livid. I would have tried to convince him he deserved better. I would have told him he shouldn't go off to basic training, that he owed the military nothing. Why should he risk his life for a country that had deserted him? Why did no one in her family try to stop either brother? How could they have been so blindly patriotic? And why is it that I can only see their loyalty as irrational and even lamentable?

These are questions I cannot sort out aloud, and issues I cannot take up with Obaachan. She would feel criticized somehow, and, more importantly, misunderstood. She would smack her lips in that disapproving way and shake her head in frustration. And because she believed at the time that it was her duty as an American citizen to get hauled out of Los Angeles without a complaint, my failure to sympathize and understand might even seem to belittle what she sacrificed. She might shut down, and refuse to tell me the rest of her story. So I keep these thoughts to myself. I must tread with caution this trail of memory we are following, or I could lose it altogether. Obaachan could close the door and let the dust settle over these years once more, and leave me with no way of knowing what happened.

In Florida, later that afternoon, Obaachan steps from the house and into the courtyard, where I am stretched out on a chaise lounge, dozing off, a worn copy of *The Catcher in the Rye* in hand. She shuffles past me and inspects the bird-of-paradise, bright orange and purple, arcing just above her head. She stands on her tiptoes and peers out at the cul-de-sac, then turns around, announces that she is heading to the library, and asks if there is anything she can pick up for me. I shake my head.

"When will you be back?" I ask. It is a question I have inherited from my parents, one they've always asked. A nervous question.

She shrugs, frowning, mildly irritated. "I won't be long. It's not far. You don't need to be concerned. Like I told your mother, I don't want to be on a schedule for other people." She smiles a little then, a half apology for her impatience, and asks me again if I want her to pick up a book or a movie. The library loans DVDs, she explains, pronouncing each letter carefully, and she has a DVD player that she has figured out how to use. I tell her I don't need anything. She walks to the garage and climbs into her silver Toyota, a gift she has recently received from her youngest son, my uncle Jay. It is the first new car she has ever owned.

That night, when I call my mother, I tell her about the conversation in the courtyard. She sighs and attempts to explain my grandmother's response. Don't take it personally, she insists, her voice firm and soothing. (My mother is much tougher than I and rarely takes anything personally. Of course she knows this difference between us, and feels she must try to convince me not to be hurt.)

Once, when she was visiting Obaachan, she explains, she had pressed my grandmother in a similar way, for an estimated time of return.

Obaachan shook her head in frustration. There was no need to worry; she was fine on her own. My mother, in one final attempt to get a return time, tried reminding my grandmother that she was eighty years old.

"Yes," Obaachan replied, "and for the first time in my life, I can go anywhere I want without having to answer to someone, without having to keep checking my watch. Your father always kept me on a schedule. We had to have dinner at a certain hour. We had to water the garden at a specific time. And when he was sick, it was even worse. There were only ninety minutes on each oxygen tank. Every time I left the house, I had to keep track of those minutes. And every time I came home, I'd hope that I hadn't somehow made a mistake. That he wouldn't have run out of air. So don't ask me when I'll be home, please. I don't have to be home for anybody these days, not the government, not my husband, and not even you. And that's the way I like it."

On the phone my mother tells me again that I have to decide not to take it personally. "Your grandmother has been ordered around her whole life," she says. "Where to go, when to be home. She was never free to do what she wanted, not until recently. Picture yourself in her shoes, honey. Try to understand."

Three days before Christmas of 1941, *Life* magazine ran an article titled "How to Tell Japs from the Chinese." The article presented photographs of two men, one Japanese and one Chinese, placed side by side. There were arrows drawn with handwritten notes describing the differences in the facial features of the two men. My grandmother's family did not have the money to subscribe to magazines, and Mama and Papa did not read English, so they would not have had this issue in their home. However, Obaachan walked around Los Angeles all the time, and she would have passed news-stands on the streets downtown, and seen articles like this. I imagine she cringed at the photographs and notes. It was hard not to feel *haji* when she saw these things and let the hate of those words sink in.

However, aside from a handful of upsetting articles and headlines, life did not drastically change in those early weeks after Pearl Harbor, at least not for those Japanese who, like my grandmother, were American citizens. Other than being prohibited from leaving the country—which was, of course, a significant violation of their freedom—their constitutional rights had not yet been curtailed. But the *Issei*, or first-generation Japanese, faced a different situation. Obaachan's parents were *Issei*. Born in Japan and not legally permitted to become naturalized citizens, they were now "enemy aliens" living in a country that was at war with their homeland. And because they were enemy aliens, the government froze their bank accounts and other liquid assets. In more ways than one, they were trapped.

And yet, on Christmas morning, Obaachan's family celebrated as they always had: they exchanged a few small gifts and went to church. The pastor read from the book of Luke, and the children collected their tiny white boxes of chocolate on their way out the front door. New Year's, too, for them was much like it had been in years past. For Japanese families, New Year's was a much more significant holiday than Christmas. The observance of Christmas had been adopted in America; it was a Christian holiday that they hadn't celebrated in their home country. New Year's, on the other hand, involved much older traditions, and was a day steeped in generations of customs.

Obaachan spent most of New Year's Day orchestrating her family's dinner, just as she had the previous two years. Her mother, still wanting to be a part of the event, lay on her bed, calling out questions and instructions. Preparing the *tai*, or snapper, was a tedious ordeal. First, the body of the fish had to be slit with a sharp knife to ensure that the oven heat would penetrate it evenly. Then the tail had to be curved back into an arch and made to stick up in the air. It was fastened between two slices of *daikon* with a toothpick. The ridges of the fin were separated, and again, a *daikon* was placed on either side.

Obaachan also cooked black soybeans with *shoyu* and sugar, plus red adzuki beans. She made *sushi,* steaming the rice and mixing in the sugar and vinegar, then fanning it to give it a sheen. She knelt in Papa's garden and cut bamboo shoots, then carefully sliced them and added them to the carrots and little *imo* potatoes, which she cooked with *dashi*, a soup base that gave it a rich flavor. For dessert there was *mochi*, the bulbous rice flour pastry that Obaachan had purchased the day before at a Japanese grocery store. And of course, all of the food was accompanied with *sake.*

But the meal was only one aspect of the holiday. For Obaachan's family, New Year's was not a time for drinking champagne and making a whimsical list of resolutions. It was a day for reflecting, for thinking about the year that had passed. It was also a time for looking ahead to the future. All disputes were to be settled, and all debts paid. These were not things to be carried into the New Year like baggage; they weighed people down and prevented them from living fully.

In this spirit of forgiveness and renewal, Japanese families visited friends and neighbors. Because she was confined to her bed, Mama could not participate in much of the holiday, and out of respect for her, very few people came to the house, preferring to give her her privacy. But Papa made his rounds, cruising through the neighborhood to wish the families he knew a happy year to come. It was a day of new beginnings. A day of hope.

Through the 1941 holiday season, however, a degree of uncertainty must have hung over their celebrations. Although my grandmother's family cooked the same traditional meals and participated in the same customs they always had, at the back of their minds, they had to be wondering what the year 1942 had in store for them. After all, they knew that many Japanese families had not been so fortunate as to spend December without trouble. While none of their close friends were affected, Obaachan and her parents learned of what was happening on their radio, in the *Rafu Shimpo* newspaper, and through the stories that circulated around the community with increasing frequency. All along the West Coast, Japanese fishing vessels were intercepted by officers of the Immigration and Naturalization Service. The fishermen were escorted to land and questioned; some were arrested. Community leaders, Buddhist priests, teachers—essentially anyone in a leadership position in the community—could be considered suspicious. Across Los Angeles, houses were searched by armed men in the middle of the night, and husbands and brothers were handcuffed and hauled off without explanation. Overall, around seven thousand individuals were arrested in this initial roundup.

Friends of my grandmother's family began getting rid of belongings that might imply disloyalty: paintings from Japan, for example, or tiny statues of Buddha. They also draped American flags from their porches, hung pictures of great patriots like Washington and Lincoln on their walls, and posted signs that claimed in bold capital letters, "I AM AN AMERICAN" in their storefronts. Obaachan's family had few relics from Japan, so they had little to take down or throw away. There was the statue of the emperor her mother placed in the living room for holidays. The emperor was a religious figure as much as a political one, but certainly, having a statue of the Japanese ruler in the home could have been misconstrued as treasonous. The family also had a set of painted dolls that were set up on display on Girls' Day, March 3, and Boys' Day, May 5. (Japanese believe even numbers to be bad luck and avoid them with great effort, hence the odd-numbered dates of these holidays. My mother, who claims to disdain all acts of superstition, still insists on making three or five *sushi* rolls, not four or six.)

For the most part, however, the attempts of the Japanese to show loyalty to America were disregarded. As New Year's shifted into mid-January and then February, *hakujin* paranoia and anger heightened. The flags, portraits, and signs were insignificant. Citizenship, too, became irrelevant. What mattered was the dark hair and slanted eyes—and the treachery assumed to be behind those eyes. Soon, my grandmother's family would realize just how little their patriotism mattered to the *hakujin* who controlled their fate.

In fact, with each passing day of 1942, it became more and more impossible to ignore the brewing hostility and anxiety that many California whites felt toward their Japanese neighbors. General John L. DeWitt, the newly appointed commander of the Western Defense Command, the man who eventually orchestrated the mass evacuation, made it clear how he felt about all people of Japanese descent: "A Jap's a Jap. It makes no difference whether he is an American citizen or not." Similar sentiments were reflected all across the media—and my grandmother, if not her parents, would have read the headlines and heard the accounts. Henry McLemore, a syndicated newspaper columnist, told his readers:

> I am for immediate removal of every Japanese on the West Coast to a point deep in the interior. I don't mean a nice part of the interior either. Herd 'em up, pack 'em off and give 'em the inside room in the badlands. Let 'em be pinched, hurt, hungry and dead up against it . . . Personally, I hate the Japanese. And that goes for all of them.

A journalist in Obaachan's city echoed these feelings in the *Los Angeles Times* on February 2: "A viper is nonetheless a viper wherever the egg is hatched. So a Japanese-American . . . grows up to be a Japanese, not an American." And on February 12, Fletcher Bowron, the mayor of my grandmother's beloved hometown, said, in a special radio broadcast in honor of Lincoln's birthday, "There isn't a shadow of a doubt but that Lincoln, the mild-mannered man whose memory we regard with almost saintlike reverence, would make short work of rounding up the Japanese and putting them where they could do no harm." With so many prominent individuals making such strong pronouncements, it was only a matter of time before action was taken against the Japanese living on the West Coast.

In the early months of 1942, the authorities started urging Japanese families to leave their West Coast homes and move east, away from the volatile Pacific. They called it a "voluntary evacuation," implying that those folks who chose to leave would be doing so for their own safety. But, with their financial resources frozen, how were these Japanese, whose mere appearance by this point both frightened and enraged many *hakujin* Americans, supposed to relocate and start over? How much success would they find in wandering into, say, an Oklahoma town, and attempting to open a business and buy a house? They seemed to be doomed from the start. Still, despite their poor odds, around nine thousand of them did attempt to follow the government's recommendations, packing up their vehicles with essentials and heading east.

Obaachan's family did not try this voluntary evacuation. Instead, they stayed put, which, it turned out, was for the best. Those families who attempted to leave on their own were met with hostility, and all across Los Angeles, accounts of failed attempts were whispered about and passed along. My grandmother no doubt heard these stories. In her neighborhood, she could have learned of someone who'd been forced back by armed posses at the border of Nevada. At the store down the street, tales of others who'd been locked up overnight by nervous local officials. And in Little Tokyo, a story of a young man who'd been refused fuel by three gas stations, and who'd eventually turned back with his wife.

Having realized that the voluntary evacuation had not panned out as they'd hoped, the government began formulating alternative plans. On March 2, General John L. DeWitt declared the entire West Coast a military zone. A few weeks later, on March 27, the Five-Mile Curfew was enacted. Although the curfew technically applied to all enemy aliens living in that military zone—that is, the Germans and Italians, along with the Japanese—it was easier to enforce it on the Japanese. They looked different, and so were an easy target, whereas the Germans and Italians blended in with most other *hakujin*.

Essentially, the curfew was a set of rules regulating when and where enemy aliens could go. It restricted them from traveling beyond a five-mile radius of their homes unless they were going to or from their place of employment, or evacuating from the military zone. The curfew also mandated that enemy aliens never leave their homes between the hours of 9:00 p.m. and 6:00 a.m. Obaachan's father, who left for work at the produce market during these forbidden hours, was supposedly safe as long as he could prove he was going to work by showing the appropriate papers. But if, for some reason, he'd seemed suspicious, or if he'd failed to provide sufficient evidence of his shift hours and place of employment, he would've been arrested. His family would not have been told where he'd been taken.

Obaachan's Papa prided himself on being a law-abiding man, though, so he stressed the importance of obeying the rules, even if they seemed unnecessary or unfair. In fact, he never said whether or not he agreed with the laws; he simply emphasized the value of respecting them. "A nation cannot thrive if people decide to create their own rules," he'd told his children when they were young. "Your mother and I chose to move to this country, and we must be willing to follow its laws." He and Mama had taken great care to raise their family with this mind-set.

The Five-Mile Curfew, while inconvenient, did not do much to hinder my grandmother's existence, and it was relatively easy for her and her family to adjust to its demands. Mama, with her heart condition, rarely left the house to begin with. Papa simply had to make sure he had the appropriate paperwork with him on his way to and from work. Obaachan would not have dared to venture out in the dark alone anyway. It was far too dangerous, and she was far too timid to risk being a victim of one of the random assaults on Japanese she kept hearing about on her daytime trips to Little Tokyo.

Shortly after the Five-Mile Curfew was passed, though, a more troubling announcement was made: all people of Japanese ancestry were to go to the police and hand in their guns, swords, and shortwave radios. Whereas most people did not put up much of a fuss regarding the Five-Mile Curfew, at least not those my grandmother knew, this new decree created more of a stir. Back then, listening to the radio was the best way to learn what was going on outside the local area. For Obaachan's parents, their shortwave radio was a vital connection to the world because it could pick up stations from Japan, which of course featured announcers who spoke their native language. Unable to understand or read much English, her parents depended on the reports they picked up on that radio, their primary means of staying up to date on the world's news.

However, as soon as Obaachan's father learned about the order to hand in all weapons and radios, he pulled the plug of his radio from the wall. Without a word of frustration, he wrapped the cord into neat folds and secured it to the back of the radio with a piece of brown twine. He grabbed his fedora hat, the one he wore in the winter months, tucked the radio under his arm, and headed for the police station to turn it in.

Though few Japanese families possessed guns and even fewer owned swords, those who did have a *samurai* sword hanging on a living-room wall were forced to give up something of great sentimental value. Obaachan's family did not have any—they were not from that social class—but she was still aware of the significance of these swords. In addition to their monetary value, *samurai* swords were family heirlooms. In Japan, the *samurai* always came from the highest social class, and so having a sword to hang on the wall was not only a piece of history but also a status symbol, a reminder of a family's high social rank in the old land.

A few *Nisei*, or second-generation Japanese, mostly young men educated in American universities, pointed out in *Rafu Shimpo* editorials that as US citizens, they had the right to bear arms according to the Constitution. The government ignored the argument, which did not inspire protests or civil disobedience on the part of Japanese Americans or their neighbors. And things were only going to get worse. By March 30, the option of evacuating voluntarily came to an end; General DeWitt announced that all people of Japanese ancestry were strictly prohibited from leaving the military zone. They were ordered to stay put until "arrangements" were made.

Chapter 3

ON MY SECOND TRIP TO FLORIDA, A YEAR LATER,
Obaachan announces that to celebrate my twenty-third
birthday, she is taking me to a Thai restaurant a few
miles south of her house, a place she has been to once
and thinks I will like. We are seated on a second level,
one that allows a bird's-eye view of the entire restaurant, and right beside us is a giant saltwater fish tank.
Obaachan knows that she will order the Goong Gah
Tiem, or garlic shrimp, which is what she had last time,
with my uncle Jay. I have more trouble deciding among
the many choices and try to read quickly through the
detailed descriptions.

"My uncle Kisho used to own a restaurant,"
Obaachan says, closing her menu. "A Chinese one, not
Japanese. Before the war."

"Chinese?" I say, a little perplexed. Japanese people are notoriously snooty about their food. Once, my mother discovered a bottle of La Choy in my refrigerator, and reproached me for buying Chinese soy sauce. Japanese people buy Japanese products, she explained, frustrated by my offense. I should know better. A week later, she handed me a new bottle of Kikkoman.

"People liked Chinese food more than Japanese, I guess," Obaachan continues. "It's probably still true. You see Chinese restaurants just about everywhere, and even though more and more *hakujin* eat *sushi* nowadays, Japanese restaurants are not as common."

Obaachan's father and Uncle Kisho had come to America together, the only members of their family to leave Japan, and they shared a close relationship. Her father was the older of the two, and like many Japanese immigrants at the time, he married the woman his parents had arranged for him. But Uncle Kisho had done things differently. Perhaps the idea of waiting for his picture bride to arrive at a designated American harbor had not appealed to him as it had to Obaachan's father. Instead, Uncle Kisho saved his money, opened his restaurant, and waited, confident that in time, the perfect woman would come along. Eventually he met Maki, right there in Los Angeles.

When Uncle Kisho met Maki, her life was in shambles. Her first husband had died, and she was left to care for four daughters all alone. "I have no idea how she managed," Obaachan says, shaking her head. "They didn't have life insurance policies back then, and I don't know how she would've supported *and* raised a family on her own." Obaachan seems somewhat hesitant to discuss these relatives, but I'm curious and probe a little. After Maki married Uncle Kisho, all four of her daughters were sent back to Japan to be raised by a relative. (My grandmother does not know why the daughters did not stay in America, but she admits this arrangement seems a little odd.) The eldest committed suicide. (When I press for more information about this young woman, Obaachan offers this: "She was a little bit retarded, I think." When I ask her what she means by *retarded*, she shrugs. "I don't know. She was different. Something was different about her.") Later, when the remaining three were in the United States, the second daughter ran off with a boyfriend, a guy who worked at Uncle Kisho's restaurant. Uncle Kisho had to track her down and bring her home. Then he arranged a marriage—not to the man she'd run off with, but to another man.

"It was very Japanese, what he did," Obaachan says, taking her cloth napkin and placing it in her lap. "And it was what any Japanese father would have done back then. You didn't just run off like that." Doing so only brought shame to the family. There were customs that you were expected to follow. Proper procedures. Even if a marriage wasn't formally arranged, there were certain steps that had to lead up to it, like asking a representative to vouch for your respectability and integrity. "Poor Uncle Kisho. He and Aunt Maki had a lot of sadness in life. A lot of disappointment. Right before the evacuation, Kisho sold his restaurant. Probably for a pittance."

The server, a slim man with shiny black hair, returns to our table to take our order, his hands folded together formally, his face attentive. Obaachan tells him what she wants, and I request the Pad Ga Pow, stir-fried chicken with basil. He smiles, his crooked teeth large and bright, and promises that we will not be disappointed with our decisions. He looks at my grandmother. "Especially you," he says. "The Goong Gah Tiem is one of our finest dishes."

Dinner at the Thai restaurant, though not all that extravagant, is an outing my grandmother has likely had to save for. She is not in the most comfortable of financial situations at this point in her life, and she lives frugally and cautiously to ensure that she does not run out of money. Her children take care of her—my uncle paid for her car and my aunt bought the house she lives in—but I believe she accepts these gifts only because she has no choice. She has arrived, as she likes to say, at the age when her children now tell her what to do.

In March of 1942, Obaachan's father began urging Uncle Kisho to sell the Chinese restaurant while he still could and then move into the house on Pico Street so they could all be together. For some time only three people had been living in the house, Obaachan and her parents, so there was lots of room. When Uncle Kisho and Aunt Maki and her two youngest daughters moved in, that raised the total to seven. Shortly thereafter, Obaachan's sister, Sachiko, and her husband moved in, too. Eight and a half months pregnant at the time, Sachiko was due with her first child any day.

I can imagine my own father doing the same thing, were he in a similar situation, gathering together what pieces of his family he could, trying to maintain a sense of calm and solidarity during a stressful time. Obaachan's two brothers were no longer in Los Angeles. By this point, Ren, the one who'd been asked to resign from Fresno Air Force Base, had been drafted by the US Army and had left for basic training in Arkansas, and Jack, Obaachan mentions briefly, was also gone.

"Where was Jack?" I ask.

She looks away and mumbles that she does not remember, which I sense is not entirely true, but when I press her for answers, she reminds me, peering over her glasses and looking at me sternly, that we agreed not to talk much about the siblings. She takes a deep breath, pausing, so that her silence holds its weight with me. "I was telling you about the house," she says then, shifting my attention to a subject more comfortable for her. "Sure, it was crowded, with nine of us living there," she says. "But we knew it was temporary. By that time we understood that we would not be in LA for long, and we figured they would send us off by the household. Papa believed that if we were under the same roof, we would have a better chance of getting sent to the same place."

The server passes, slowing and glancing at our glasses to make sure that we haven't run out of water, and says the food will be out in just a few minutes. He smiles and continues to a nearby table, again with his hands folded in his official style. He begins to take their order, nodding and repeating each request. Obaachan takes a sip of her water, trying to avoid the ice because it hurts her teeth, and looks at me from across the table. "In other words, if we had to leave our home, we wanted to leave it together."

In the end, her father was right: families were evacuated by the household. But there was a hitch in his plan that he hadn't anticipated. Just after Sachiko had her baby, she and her husband announced that they were leaving for Sacramento to be with her husband's family. Although Obaachan's father might have been devastated to learn that he would be separated from his daughter and new grandson, he knew that in Japanese families, the husband's word—even if that husband was a son-in-law—was not to be questioned. He did not oppose their decision.

"I got to meet my little nephew before we were sent away," Obaachan says, "but then, as soon as my sister recovered, the three of them moved out. They didn't say much except that their plans had changed. That's how they ended up in Arkansas during the war," Obaachan explains. "They went with his family, not ours."

For the next few years, the only thing that would allow my grandmother to stay in touch with her sister was letters—letters that were, in accordance with military protocol, always opened and read by the authorities before they were delivered. Knowing this, I think I begin to understand a little better the detached relationships my grandmother now shares with her siblings. For some, hardship and separation create a special bond, a closeness that cannot be understood by outsiders. This didn't happen with my grandmother and her family. Instead, they seem to have drifted apart during the war, and the rift never repaired itself. Although her sister and two brothers are still alive, Obaachan corresponds sparingly with them: Christmas and birthday cards are their only communication. The evacuation splintered the family, much more permanently than they might have imagined back in 1942. Their letters would not be enough to hold them together.

Across every city in the new "military zone," posters were stapled to telephone poles and taped to store windows. Labeled "Instructions to All Persons of Japanese Ancestry," they applied to anyone with as little as one-sixteenth Japanese blood. These instructions were also listed in the newspapers, and Papa, who could only read Japanese, read them in the *Rafu Shimpo*. Dated April 1, 1942, the instructions stated that everyone would be removed from the designated areas by noon of April 7. Obaachan's family had six days to pack. The instructions, however, were vague, raising questions that were overwhelming:

"Evacuees must carry with them on departure for the Reception Center, the following property:

    a. Bedding and linens (no mattress) for each member of the family.

    b. Toilet articles for each member of the family.

    c. Extra clothing for each member of the family.

    d. Sufficient knives, forks, spoons, plates, bowls and cups for each member of the family.

    e. Essential personal effects for each member of the family . . ."

But what kind of extra clothing should they take? Heavy winter coats or lightweight summer dresses? What were "essential personal effects"? And how many toiletries would they need exactly? To make things more difficult, each person was limited to what he or she could carry in terms of how many parcels. No extra luggage was permitted.

At last the server returns with our food, one hot plate in each hand. He places the garlic shrimp in front of Obaachan, and then sets down my Pad Ga Pow. The sweet smells of shallots and basil pour off my plate. The chicken, with its savory sauce and scattered bell peppers, looks delicious. Obaachan gushes over the meal, tells the server she was here a few months back, with her son, and that today we're celebrating my birthday. The server makes a slight bow, grins, and backs away. For a few minutes, we eat in silence, enjoying the unusual blends of flavors.

Then, Obaachan chuckles as she remembers something. "What I recall being most anxious about with the packing was the "toiletries" part. We thought about sanitary napkins, and we were terrified by the prospect of running out. We bought *hundreds* of them!" She and the two cousins went out and bought large pieces of canvas and then sewed them into giant sacks. They filled each one with sanitary napkins, stuffing it with as many thick white pads as they could. "We didn't know if we'd be able to buy them where we went. We didn't know anything." She sighs. "You just had to guess, and try to prepare as best you could."

Her mother's heart condition further complicated those preparations. First, there was the decision as to whether or not she should even go along. Her doctors had spoken with the authorities and had obtained special permission for her to stay behind in Los Angeles. She would simply live in the hospital as a long-term patient. To an extent, knowing Mama was in the hands of qualified physicians would be reassuring to Papa. After all, there might not be doctors, hospitals, clean facilities, or beds where they were going. The conditions might be too harsh; the weather, too severe. In fact, the trip itself might be too much for her. The doctors had warned from the start that even under the strictest supervision and the most ideal circumstances, Mama's weak heart would not last long.

But on the other hand, the idea of leaving her behind was deeply unsettling; there was no guarantee that they would or *could* come back. Ever. And in the meantime, would the family be able to keep in touch with her? If her health grew worse, would someone contact Papa? Would he be able to come say goodbye? Would the family ever see her again? In the end Papa decided that Mama should not stay behind. Despite the risks involved in what might lie ahead, having her close to him and knowing he could be there for her if she needed him was most important.

On one of the six afternoons they had to prepare for their departure, Papa and Uncle Kisho went shopping at a department store downtown and picked up matching winter coats for their wives: thick, gray ones with fur collars. Although they did not know whether they would actually need them, the possibility of facing a winter without a warm coat was not a challenge they were willing to ask their wives to risk. Obaachan's father also picked up some metal camping plates and an electric hot plate. These articles, along with the sheets, towels, and clothing, were added to the suitcases. Item by item, the family was checking off the list.

But packing was only one part of preparing to leave. The house, the furniture, the belongings that could not be carried—arrangements had to be made for all of these things. While many people chose to store their furniture and appliances in government-run warehouses, Papa wanted to avoid having to do that. The posted instructions made it clear that there would be no guarantees regarding items left in those warehouses: "The United States Government through its agencies will provide for the storage *at the sole risk of the owner* of the more substantial household items, such as iceboxes, washing machines, pianos and other heavy furniture . . ." What that meant, Papa understood, was that there was no way of knowing whether those things would be there when he returned.

Instead, he found a tenant to rent his house, fully furnished: a minister, an African American man whose church was nearby. As soon as the family found out where they would be sent and what their mailing address would be, Papa would contact the minister. For his part, the minister promised to send the agreed-upon amount each month by a certain date. Papa felt good about the deal. Compared to many Japanese, who had no choice but to sell off their farms and belongings for far less than their worth, he had not made such a bad arrangement.

"None of our non-Japanese neighbors were willing to help," Obaachan says, shaking her head and setting her fork on her plate. "They wouldn't store things for us, or assist in any way. These were people we'd known for years, people who'd watched my siblings and me grow up. But all of a sudden, they wanted nothing to do with us. We were on our own."

Like Obaachan's father, Mama, too, had her decisions to make. Although she was not a sentimental woman, she insisted on holding on to her Noritake china, the lovely white set her parents had sent from Japan as a wedding gift. She would not, as her friends and neighbors did, sell something so valuable for a meager amount, nor would she smash them to pieces, as some desperate women did in a flurry of spite. She would not give them up if she could help it. Papa, always resourceful, found a church that was willing to store his wife's beloved china.

"My sister has it all now," Obaachan says with a smile. "She showed it to me the last time I went to visit her, in LA, a few years ago. My mother never made it back to the West Coast, you know, but Sachiko must have gone to the church and picked up Mama's china, after the war." Her voice quiets at this memory. The irony is still painful. "It's strange, what survives, and what doesn't."

The day of evacuation finally arrived. April sunshine tumbled auspiciously on the yard, and the forsythias Papa had spent years caring for bloomed in bright yellow splashes in front of the house. Mama, using a smooth black cane Aunt Maki had purchased from a family friend, stepped cautiously off the porch. Obaachan held on to her mother's arm, supporting her. Mama's hair was twisted into a bun at the nape of her neck, and she wore a gray tweed suit. Papa made one last trip through each room of the house, doing a final check, or maybe saying goodbye to all that he had worked for.

At the sidewalk, the minister waited with his wife. Papa handed him the keys, and the minister reminded Obaachan to send him their new address as soon as she learned what it was. Because her father could not read or write in English, Obaachan would be the one responsible for corresponding with the minister. The men shook hands, and Papa managed a muffled "thank you" in English, one of the few phrases he knew. As they reached the corner of the lot, Obaachan took a final look at the house, and then at Mama, who seemed tired already, leaning on her cane. The minister's wife raised her arm in a wave. Papa never turned back.

Each area of each city was assigned a specific meeting place, a building or parking lot where the families needed to be by noon on April 7, with all packed belongings in hand. It was all detailed on the posted instructions.

"Ours was the church where my family attended," Obaachan says. She leans back in her chair, then dabs her lips with her napkin and takes a sip of water. "It was strange, of course, going to a place you knew well, and had been to many times before, but under such different circumstances."

The seven of them shuffled the few blocks to the church, the sewn knapsacks slung over one shoulder, the suitcases gripped in the opposite hand. Papa carried Mama's things. In the parking lot a few hundred people gathered, and they huddled together in quiet clusters. Papa and Uncle Kisho went to stand in line and register their families. "We became numbers at that point," Obaachan says, cutting a shrimp in half and swirling it in the sauce. She leans back in her chair. "You were registered as a number, not as a name."

A pair of scales was set up at the registration table, and a stern group of burly, uniformed men roughly picked up each suitcase and slammed it onto a scale. Those who had brought too much luggage were treated with cold impatience and commanded to remove items from their bags until the required weight was reached. These belongings were left scattered on the street outside the church, and they were scavenged the moment the buses pulled out of the parking lot. Today, photographs of these meeting places—with open suitcases, clothing, musical instruments, and other items tossed about, and *hakujin* looking for things worth keeping after the busloads of Japanese had been carried away—capture the event.

At first Obaachan's Mama tried to stand in the church parking lot, but before long she grew too tired. She sat on the concrete steps that led to the church entrance. Other women sat in circles nearby. Red Cross workers carried trays of coffee through the crowd, as if offering comfort in a natural disaster.

Finally, buses with armed military police pulled up. Standing outside the bus, gripping their rifles and looking straight ahead, the police ordered everyone aboard. At this point still not knowing where they were headed, hundreds of people filed into the buses. Obedient, quiet. "Nobody resisted," Obaachan remembers. "I think people had the mind-set that this was what we could do to help. We loved America just like everyone else, and if this was the way we could serve our country, we were willing to do it. We saw it as our duty."

The Japanese American Citizens League, a civil rights organization consisting of only *Nisei* (those who were American citizens), had encouraged people to believe this though the discriminatory legislation continued. Their creed, written in 1940, included these words: "Because I believe in America, and I trust she believes in me, and because I have received innumerable benefits from her, I pledge myself to do honor to her at all times and all places . . . in the hope that I may become a better American in a greater America." After the bombing of Pearl Harbor, the JACL had pledged loyalty to the United States while condemning the treachery of Japan. When a mandatory evacuation was announced, they urged the Japanese to leave without resistance—to do their duty by obeying the rules.

The *Nisei* who made up the JACL would have been young, optimistic folks, some of them college educated. I can't help thinking about the 1960s, when twenty-somethings protested the Vietnam War and the government, and about now, when my friends march at anti–death penalty rallies and insist on buying fair trade coffee. Were this type of roundup to happen in my own day, I feel confident that my generation—my post–civil rights, optimistic, unafraid generation—would unite to oppose what it would undoubtedly deem unjust. But, as my grandmother has pointed out to me, we did not grow up in the same world.

As the caravan of buses drove through the city of Los Angeles that April day, people stopped to stare. Some pointed and a few yelled. "You don't belong here!" hollered a middle-aged man. "Dirty Japs!" shouted a young girl. "This is what you deserved!" yelled a mother, holding her infant son to her chest.

Even though my grandmother had always lived in, and was quite accustomed to, a country that resented her race—even though she had seen all the headlines and heard the radio reports with their accusations and assumptions—she had never felt so despised as she did riding through Los Angeles that April afternoon. She was ashamed to be Japanese. She was ashamed to be American.

At the Thai restaurant, when we've at last filled our stomachs and scraped what we couldn't finish of our meal into two Styrofoam boxes, Obaachan takes out her red wallet and places a few crisp bills on the table. Offering to cover the tip would offend her. This dinner, she reminds me, is my birthday gift. I thank her again for the outing, and we walk to the car. Whenever she has visitors, my grandmother does not drive. Although she has never had an accident, she prefers sitting in the passenger seat to driving, especially at night. She hands me the keys. I push the button to unlock all the doors, and help her into the car. Sometimes, the seatbelt is difficult for her to reach on that side.

We pull out of the parking lot and head home. In the hour or so we have spent at the restaurant, Melbourne has grown dark. The bright lights of strip malls illuminate the sides of the road: dry cleaners, 7–Elevens, banks, and real estate agencies flash past.

From the floor of the backseat, our leftovers are beginning to soak the air with their heavy scent. Beside me, my eighty-year-old grandmother holds her purse on her lap, her hands resting on its top. She is quiet now, tired from a long day of remembering, and ready to head home.

Chapter 4

ON THE FINAL DAY OF MY SECOND TRIP TO FLORIDA, Obaachan asks me to help her pick the grapefruit. Outside the kitchen window, in the small patch of yard between her house and the row of shrubs lining the road stand two trees that she and my grandfather planted when they first moved here, in 1989. Each now stretches over twelve feet tall and has wide branches with thick, shiny leaves. Swollen yellow fruit, dusted with a chalky black substance, burdens the branches, and they sag a little from the weight.

"We'll need this," Obaachan says, pointing to a four-foot wooden ladder in a corner of the garage. I grab it, haul it awkwardly to the closest tree, and set it up, checking its strength by trying to rock it back and forth in the grass. Obaachan places a cardboard box once used to haul Dole bananas on the ground at the foot of the tree. "The kind they use for bananas are the best," she explains. "The sturdiest."

Like Obaachan's Papa, my grandfather, too, had always been interested in growing things; he'd helped my aunt create a colossal vegetable garden at her Maryland home, where he and Obaachan had lived for a while before moving south. "I can't keep up with them," Obaachan says, pointing to the branches and the hundreds of heavy grapefruits that hang from them. "Even if I ate two or three a day, I couldn't. I'm sending a box home with you, for your mother. And for you, if you want some. It's easy to take them. You just tape up the box and check it with your other luggage." Her other spring visitor, my uncle Jay, has recently taken a shipment of grapefruit home to Denver.

I climb the ladder, a little wary of its creaking wooden rungs, and then heave myself onto a branch. Obaachan slides the cardboard box a few feet along the ground so that it's resting just below my perch. I pull at the first grapefruit, feel it firm and full in my fingertips. I twist it just a bit until it gives and then drop it into the box. It weighs nearly a pound, and lands loudly on the cardboard.

Since dinner at the Thai restaurant two nights earlier, Obaachan and I have not talked about the evacuation. We've watched *The Four Feathers* and the original *Sabrina* and taken advantage of her senior citizen's discount at the nearby Ross store. I've introduced her to chai lattes, and she has taught me how to make perfect popcorn on the stovetop. All of this has been fun, and throughout all of it, I've been surprised by just how easy it has been to spend a week with a woman I still feel I don't know that well. We have a good bit in common, I've realized. We both like reading, watching movies, and cooking, and we've enjoyed exchanging recipes and book recommendations. But I begin to worry that she has decided she has talked enough already—that she has exposed too much. I feel that she has gotten to know me this week, but I sense that there's still so much I don't know about her. And, as she warned me from the very beginning, she does not like to talk about herself.

I worry, too, that although we have managed to navigate through the easier details of childhood, through the years before the war and the camp, the difficult memories lie ahead, and I wonder if my grandmother will find reasons to shift our conversations to something other than the war itself. Backward, to those early years on Pico Street, in her Papa's giant garden; or ahead, far ahead, to the quiet years in southern New Jersey, after the war, when she and my grandfather were busy raising four children. I realize I must find a way to dive back into the story, right to where we left off a few days ago. "When you left Los Angeles and got on that bus," I call to her from the branches of the grapefruit tree, trying to defuse the question by tossing a grapefruit into the box, "did you go straight to Wyoming?"

She doesn't answer. I wait nervously in the branches above her, yanking fruit with both hands, holding to the tree with my legs. I fear I'm pushing her too much.

Obaachan steps to her left so that she can get a clear view of me through the branches, and looks up, shielding her eyes from the sun. "The real camps weren't built yet. We didn't get to Heart Mountain until months later." She hesitates for a moment to think about the timeline, to sift through the days and figure how long it really was. She pulls a grapefruit from a low branch, turns it in her hands, rubbing a little at the black substance. "It wasn't until August, I think. For those months in between, we were at Pomona."

Named after the ancient Roman goddess of fruit, the city of Pomona was a little town originally known for its fertile land and its abundant fruit trees. Thirty miles west of Los Angeles, it offered a perfect holding spot for the Japanese. It was close enough that the prisoners could be transported there quickly, and it was far enough away from the coast to put General DeWitt and the War Relocation Authority at ease—at least until other plans were in place.

Before it became a housing project for over ten thousand Japanese evacuees, Pomona was where the

Los Angeles County Fair was held. The fairground, first constructed in 1922 as a 43-acre parcel, had continually been expanded, and by the time my grandmother got there in 1942, it had grown to 105 acres. It featured a racetrack, multiple exhibit buildings, and numerous barns. The roaring sound of horses racing, the cheers of crowds, the harvest exhibits, the gambling, the band, the smell of salt and vinegar—all of this was no doubt a welcome diversion from the hardships of the Great Depression. But when my grandmother arrived that spring, she was greeted by hundreds of military police armed with machine guns. The Army had been using the site as a base since December, right after the bombing of Pearl Harbor.

"The bus ride was short," Obaachan says, pulling another grapefruit from a low branch. "Less than an hour. Pomona was not far at all. But somehow, it was a very long trip."

The bus, though crowded, was marked by a startling silence. Even small children sat gravely in their seats, leaning against a parent, clutching a favorite doll or toy truck. A young boy played with his Slinky, its rings clinking. The buses pulled into the fairground, slowed, and quieted their engines. Everyone was ordered to exit. Obaachan's mother struggled to make her way down the aisle, and she gripped the backs of the bus seats with each step. Military police called out the numbers on each bundle or suitcase, and when Obaachan's family number was called, the seven of them gathered their belongings and headed toward the registration line. There, soldiers searched their bags for razors, flashlights, and other banned items. They unrolled Papa's bundle and examined the contents. They opened Mama's suitcase and sifted through the neatly folded clothing, feeling for sharp items in the layers. Obaachan, embarrassed when a young *hakujin* soldier rummaged through her hundreds of sanitary napkins (a perplexed look on his face), averted her eyes. She looked at her feet, the shiny black shoes already dusty from the dry fairground and all its human traffic.

Noticing Mama's condition, her weak body and breathlessness, one *hakujin* man took her aside and allowed her to sit on a stack of giant burlap rice bags. She sat down, her shoulders sagging a little from exhaustion, and kicked at a stone. After their belongings were searched and found to be satisfactory, Obaachan's family was given an apartment number and sent to pick up their mattresses. They later learned that they'd been lucky to get actual mattresses; when those ran out, the government officials distributed straw-stuffed sacks instead.

Wearily, Obaachan followed Papa and Uncle Kisho, dragging her mattress and her homemade knapsack. The rest of the family trailed behind. Hundreds of doors led into Pomona's buildings, and each of those doors had a number painted on its front. When Obaachan's family finally came to their new home, they stopped and stared—maybe bewildered, maybe too exhausted to be disappointed, maybe still as dutiful as ever. My grandmother, her parents, her aunt and uncle, and her two cousins were allotted a single twenty-by-twenty-foot room, a space they would share for the months that followed.

Living arrangements at Pomona had been created in two ways. There were barracklike buildings that had been thrown together as quickly as possible, and some of the existing fairground buildings had been partitioned into apartments as well. The barns, sheds, and exhibit buildings that had once housed cows, rabbits, horses, and other farm animals were cleaned out and transformed into homes for the prisoners. The walls dividing up these buildings into "apartments" were constructed of what appeared to be scrap wood, and they did not allow for much privacy with their wide spaces in between each board, and the gaping knots in the wood. Not only could Obaachan's family hear the people on either side of them—they could also see them. Shortly after their arrival, some families tried to patch the wide cracks with a mud and straw mixture, but Obaachan's did not bother. They strung sheets from pieces of wire and divided the apartment into three rooms: a bedroom for her parents, a bedroom for her aunt and uncle, and an open room that everyone had access to, where she and her cousins slept.

Meanwhile, just three days after my grandmother arrived at Pomona, on April 10, 1942, the infamous Bataan Death March commenced in the Philippines. On the ninth, American and Filipino troops handed over their weapons and left themselves to the mercy of Japanese soldiers—only to realize, too late, that Japan had no intentions of abiding by the Geneva Convention in their treatment of prisoners. Without food or water, and in the steaming heat of the South Pacific, over seventy thousand starving and sick Allied POWs began the grueling sixty-mile march to Camp O'Donnell. While a handful of them decided to escape and risk the jungles of Bataan, between five thousand and eleven thousand of them perished along the way. As this horror unfolded in the Pacific, my grandmother and her family unpacked their belongings and tried to settle into their new home at the fairground.

Obaachan examines the growing collection of grapefruit in the Dole box, and she picks one up and rolls it around in her hands. She presses her fingertips into the thick yellow skin and then holds it to her nose, smelling it. "At first," she says, "Pomona was sort of fun, at least for us young people." She shrugs. "I know that sounds funny, but I guess it was like summer camp or something. There were so many people my age to meet. It was exciting, sort of."

The exhilaration of meeting new people and making new friends may have been enough to temporarily distract a young person like my grandmother from the hardships that Pomona posed. Although she'd been forced to surrender her dream of attending college, she did not, at age twenty-one, have all that much to lose. She had few possessions, no money, no house, and no assets.

Her parents, on the other hand, had lost everything. The life they'd built together in America was now very much behind them, only thirty miles away, but completely out of reach. While Obaachan spent her evenings strolling around the grounds and hanging out with new friends, her father dreamed of the house on Pico Street. He'd paid cash for each piece of furniture, every appliance, lamp, tool, and tablecloth. He'd saved up to buy the house and paid extra for the double lot. Most of all, he thought of his garden. The tulips with their fleeting bursts of red. The oleanders, white and fragrant. His darling camellias. Without consistent watering, the camellias would dry out and die. Papa wondered if any part of his beloved garden, or even his beloved home, would be there upon his return—if there was a return.

What made the adjustment to Pomona even more of a strain was its layout and daily structure. The hundred-yard walk to the lavatories was no easy trip for someone like Obaachan's mother, who was supposed to stay in bed and avoid physical activity at all times. And waiting in line and eating at a mess hall proved to be difficult, as well, for those with infants and young children, who were often fussy, tired, and wary of the unfamiliar mess-hall foods.

"It was a different kind of diet," Obaachan says slowly. Beneath me, she adjusts her bright white hat with its wide, bonnetlike bill, and then tugs at another grapefruit. "It took some getting used to."

Many of their meals consisted primarily of cereal, rice, bread, canned beans, and hot dogs. The food was never spoiled, stale, or anything like that—but they were not foods Japanese typically ate. My grandmother's family, accustomed to a diet of fresh vegetables, fish, brown rice, and Japanese seasonings like *shoyu* and *dashi*, had difficulty adjusting to a bland, high-starch diet. Many of their friends suffered from diarrhea and stomach pains. Papa lost weight. Still, in those early months of incarceration, her father made it a point to remind Obaachan to be grateful, and not to complain. He pointed out that many Americans—not just Japanese but also lots of *hakujin*—had suffered through months and even years of hunger due to the Great Depression. Obaachan tried to take to heart what he told her, and his care in not mentioning his own anxiety and sense of loss must have helped shape her positive experience of Pomona.

I imagine my great-grandfather, so insistent on following the rules and repressing the urge to protest, and how he must have craved the fresh bamboo shoots from his garden, and the sweet, peppery *daikon* from the produce market. What loss he must have felt when he remembered the daffodils and crocuses, pushing through the dirt and unfolding in the patch along the side of the house. For my own father, who has gardened since before I was born, the plot of dirt that he plows and plants each year is more than a hobby or a way to grow food for the family. It's something he plans and thinks about, not just in the summer, but year-round. Months before the planting begins, when snow still covers the Pennsylvania ground, he flips through seed catalogs, calls in his orders, and maps out where the cucumbers, tomatoes, green beans, and zucchini will go. It's therapeutic, and it's a source of pride, too. I believe this is how Obaachan's Papa must have felt toward his own garden, but for him, all that he'd invested had been taken. The minister and his family now lived in the house Papa had built, and while they might have appreciated the colorful flowers in the yard or the scent of daffodils on a warm spring day, they would not have loved that small piece of land the way Papa did.

Obaachan suggests we move on to the second grapefruit tree. I climb down, sticky from the humidity, hands covered in the fruit's sooty substance, and move the ladder. The two of us drag the box, heavy now with our pickings, to the next tree's base. I head up the ladder again and find a spot where plenty of fruit are within reach.

"I think we all walked around in a trance for the first few weeks," Obaachan continues. "I've read that when people go from one culture to the next, or when some type of shocking event happens to them, they can become so overwhelmed that mentally and emotionally, they almost shut down for awhile. This is probably what happened to us."

"Culture shock," I say, dropping another grapefruit. "That's what they call it."

She nods. "But after awhile we began to settle in, establish routines. I got a job working in one of the mess halls. Those of us who were physically able were expected to contribute."

My grandmother and her fellow prisoners could choose from a variety of jobs: gardening, mowing, serving food, preparing food, cleaning the restrooms and other public areas. There were even postal workers, doctors, police officers, and electricians. Refusing to work, they all understood, might be interpreted as defiance. Obaachan's father warned them to be careful never to act in a way that might be perceived as rebellion. He believed that if his family followed the rules and complied with all requests, they would be treated better. He did not seem troubled that he'd already complied with every single one of the government's requests—handing in his radio, following the stipulations of the Five-Mile Curfew back in Los Angeles—yet he'd been forced out of his home anyway.

I take a break from picking, rest my back against a limb, stretch my legs out toward the trunk, and survey the tree. The branches are still bursting with fruit. Despite the box below, now full of heavy yellow spheres, it appears as though we've made no progress.

"I didn't mind working because it helped pass the time," Obaachan says. "And we were paid—twelve dollars a month, I think—so it was a way for me to earn and save some money. It was technically my first job," she reminds me.

Plus, it seemed that those who did not work only grew listless. The days at Pomona were long, hot, and dry. Outside, the sun was oppressive, and inside, the apartments were cramped. With no routine or commitments, depression easily set in. Even for those who did work, like my grandmother, there were many hours of free time, much more than she'd ever had back in Los Angeles.

Obaachan's job was a tedious one. For each meal, she had to arrive early, before the mess hall opened to visitors, and during that hour before prisoners began pouring through the doors, she measured out each person's serving of sugar: one teaspoon. She placed the sugar on a napkin, then folded up the edges and added it to the stacks on her tray. Later, when the prisoners passed through the cafeteria-style line, she carefully placed the folded napkin on each person's tray.

Before long more than five thousand people, most of them from the L.A. area, were crammed into the make-shift housing at Pomona, living in the tight quarters of the small rooms, shuffling through the long lines in the mess hall, and hauling their towels and shampoo to the isolated and dirty restrooms. As best they could, they settled in. After a few weeks, some ministers convinced the authorities to allow a piano to be brought into the fairground. On Sundays a number of religious people gathered together in one of two barns to sing hymns, pray, and hear verses read from the Bible. "I worked at the mess hall every day, including Sundays, during all three meals," Obaachan says as I hand her a final grape-fruit. "So I never went to church there."

The box, now packed with plump yellow fruit, can hold no more. I crawl out of the tree, gripping the trunk, my legs scraping the rough bark of the branches. Obaachan frowns, a little embarrassed, a little bemused. She views this admission—that she did not attend church—as a solemn confession, one that is not told lightly to a young and impressionable granddaughter. "I should've gone," she adds. "I'd always gone to church. Maybe it would've been, you know, encouraging to me. At least it would've been something familiar. Something from home."

But she resisted. Each week, as she headed home from her morning shift, she would hear the notes of hymns drifting from the barns, and she'd consider walking toward them. She would remember how the words of the psalms and the sound of the piano had once been so soothing to her—and yet somehow, at Pomona, the music and the words no longer held much meaning. Instead, she picked up her pace as she passed and proceeded toward the apartment. "I see now that I was disillusioned. With everything, I guess, but at the time, I didn't look at it that way. Maybe I had given up on my faith even. But I just told myself it was because of my schedule that I couldn't go."

Hearing my grandmother admit that she was disillusioned is surprising to me because so much of what she has told me has been characterized by a desire to emphasize the positives of each and every event. Her Papa was not picked up in the middle of the night after the curfew was instituted. Their family had been lucky enough to find a tenant and had not been forced to sell their home for a pittance. And Mama had been able to save her Noritake china. In all of these instances,

Obaachan's point seems to be that things could have been much worse.

There's certainly something to be said for this unending optimism—this buoyancy—characterizing this side of my family. My grandmother and her children tend to take things in stride. When a hardship arises—a job loss or a health problem—they don't dwell on their difficulties, but face them with resolve, head on. And yet, in this focusing primarily on the good, there's also a suspending of emotion, maybe even a denying. I remember once, when I was having a difficult time with my boyfriend Chris, right at the end of a semester, my aunt Charlotte sent me a note in the mail. "Be like the Japanese," she wrote. "Learn to compartmentalize." What she meant was that I should focus on what was most important: school. I could sort out my personal life later.

I tried to do what she said, tried to push my boyfriend and our argument to the back of my mind until I'd handed in my term papers and taken my final exams. I only half succeeded. I finished the semester, turned everything in on time. But I was miserable through every minute of it. As my *hakujin* father's daughter, I was hopelessly sensitive and could make myself sick with anxiety when things weren't settled. Even though I desperately wanted to, I couldn't summon that Japanese ability to rearrange my emotions and deal with them when it best suited my schedule—or not deal with them at all. I was, as this experience reminded me, only half Japanese.

At Pomona, in addition to the morning church services, another aspect to Sundays was, ironically, baseball, the American pastime. On every other day of the week, the boys and young men were only permitted to play in the evenings, after the final meal, but on Sundays, they were allowed to play all day long. After lunch, despite the tyrannical heat of midday, crowds of young and old gathered at the baseball field. Obaachan did not watch many of these games, but even from far away she could hear the crack of the wooden bat hitting the ball, and the cheer that swelled up right after it. The crowds grew especially loud when a baseball soared way out to the barbed-wire fence.

Even the guards seemed interested in the game. From their towers they would watch, their machine guns resting on their laps. When an especially good play was made, they would clap and holler their support. In these moments of excitement, when a man dashed around the bases, when a young boy sprawled into the dirt to make an impressive catch, when the crowds cried out in excitement, it was possible to forget that the world was at war, and that they were its prisoners.

For the women, the authorities arranged classes: sewing, crocheting, embroidering, and singing were just a few. Obaachan had learned basic embroidery as a child and had always enjoyed it. She and her sister would go to Woolworth's and buy white runners with patterns stamped on them, then embroider over the patterns. When she learned an embroidery class was being offered, she decided to sign up for it. To her surprise, she arrived for class on the first day and discovered that her instructor was a thin, wizened old Japanese man with fluffy gray hair. In contrast, his assistant was an attractive young girl.

"Can you believe it, Kimi? A *man*. I had never known a man who could embroider. This was 1942—men didn't do things like that!" The image of her own father—not to mention her two brothers—spending an afternoon in a quiet embroidering circle was comical. "That guy knew what he was doing, though," Obaachan says. "I don't know where he would've learned such a thing back then, but he was very good."

Most of the students in her class were better than she was, but they'd probably had more time to practice when they were young. Because Obaachan had taken over most of the cooking, cleaning, and caretaking when her mother became an invalid, her teenage years left little time for pursuing hobbies. "I made a picture of a colorful bird. A pheasant. It wasn't the best in the class

by any means, but it was an accomplishment for me."
Obaachan smiles and looks up at the grapefruit tree,
wrapping her hands around a low branch. "I put it in a
frame eventually. Your mother has it. Somewhere."

I lean over, pick up the heavy box, and carry it
through the garage and into the courtyard. Obaachan
goes into the house and gets the digital scale from
her bedroom, the one she weighs herself on every
morning. Although I know the box is not over the
seventy-pound limit—I could not lift it if it were—I
place it on the scale to appease her. Like her father,
Obaachan is meticulous about details and scrupulous
about following the rules. If the airline asks that its
passengers verify that their luggage is not over a
specified weight, an estimation is not good enough.
She makes sure to check it.

We place the lid on the box, reinforce the corners
with extra pieces of cardboard, and wrap it in yards
of packaging tape. I write my name and address on it
with a permanent marker, and we carry it to the car. I
go into the house and haul out my one other piece of
luggage, a suitcase, and its cranky wheels roll loudly
against the concrete. In a few hours, I will be heading
back to Pennsylvania, with only part of the story, with
more questions than answers, but also with an affection
for my grandmother that I didn't have two years ago,

on my initial visit. For the first time in my life, I am sad to leave her.

As I place the suitcase in the trunk, Obaachan stands to the side and watches.

"Did I tell you that it was at Pomona that I met your grandfather?" she asks suddenly.

I slide the suitcase toward the back of the trunk, shake my head, and turn to look at her. "No," I say. She hasn't said a word about my Ojichan.

She grins a little then, shrugs her shoulders, impishly almost, and shuffles out of the garage. "I guess you'll have to come back," she calls over her shoulder, "for your next installment. It's like a Victorian novel. You'll get more of the story next time." She steps out of the sunlight and into the house, her granddaughter a few steps behind.

Chapter 5

MY GRANDFATHER CAME TO LIVE IN AMERICA AS the result of one bizarre act of recklessness. He was a *Kibei*, which means that he had been born in America but raised and educated in Japan. When he was still an infant, his parents had left the United States and returned to their small fishing village on the Inland Sea, a town called Iwakuni. As a child, then, what my grandfather knew of America came from his parents' handful of stories and from what he read in newspapers. Although he was an American citizen, he planned to spend his life in Japan, a place he loved deeply. Iwakuni was an old castle town, founded in 1603, and it was and still is famous for its Kintai Bridge, with its series of five graceful arches. It stretches over the Nishiki River, which my grandfather crossed regularly. I remember him talking mostly about the cherry trees that grew along the banks of that river.

But in 1936, my grandfather's peaceful life in Yamaguchi Ken prefecture veered in an unexpected direction. He was sixteen at the time. It was spring, and my grandfather's beloved cherry trees, with their tangled dark branches and wispy pink and white flowers, were in full bloom. One afternoon, Ojichan was hanging around the schoolyard with a bunch of friends. Near the school's entrance, a large statue of a town dignitary stood, sternly watching over the proceedings of the students. Ojichan's friends were tossing stones over the fence of the schoolyard, seeing who could throw the farthest. And then one boy said to my grandfather, "I bet you can't hit the statue. I bet you can't hit him in the face." The rest of the boys joined in, taunting him, testing to see how far they could push him. For a few minutes, my grandfather tried to brush them off, ignoring their dares. But they persisted, and my grandfather—as my Obaachan would one day learn—was not one to shy away from risk. He threw the rock.

That ill-fated stone hit the statue square in its face, and with such a force that the tip of the nose flew off. For a brief moment, the boys stared in disbelief, not sure if that sharp noise of stone hitting stone had been what they'd thought it had been, but then they quickly scattered, terrified. In Japan, vandalism was no petty offense—and they knew it. Within a few days, my grandfather admitted his guilt to school officials. He must have known the consequences for such a confession. The community viewed his deed as an act of utter disregard for someone else's property, a willful show of disrespect. My grandfather was suspended from school for weeks, and his family was shunned.

Ojichan's father was ashamed to go to work; his mother was ashamed to walk down the street to the market. When my grandfather was finally permitted to return to school, he and his family realized that he was hopelessly behind. Because of the rigorous pace of Japanese schools, he would not be able to catch up and would have to accept failing grades. His father was angry with his son for his careless behavior, but also perhaps understood that Ojichan would always have the reputation of a vandal and a failure in Iwakuni, and that his life there was no longer promising. He encouraged Ojichan to leave the country. "You have no future here," he insisted. "You're an American citizen. You should go there. It's your only chance for a happy life."

Within a few months, my grandfather was headed for California on a great ship, alone, with his one rectangular leather suitcase, and the equivalent of a few dollars in his pocket. In his suitcase, he had a small stack of photographs from his life in Japan: portraits of his mother and father, a few pictures of friends, and the long bridge with its series of arches that he had crossed each day on his way to school. He was not yet seventeen years old.

As children, my brother and I heard this account many times. My grandfather would sit on the floor with us, his knees folded, his dark eyes grave yet still dancing, his hands flapping about for emphasis. Sometimes my brother, restless and lively, would sprawl across his lap as he spoke. "*Batu, batu*," Ojichan would say. Settle down, settle down.

I think my grandfather understood that his coming to America was a unique story: it was one that would interest us, but more importantly, it could be used to convey an important moral to his impressionable (and rambunctious) grandchildren. All the stories he told—and there were many, both from his life and imagination—involved some sort of lesson. Even though we children couldn't understand why vandalism was viewed with such disdain in Japan, or why my grandfather had been treated so harshly both by his community and by his own father, we grasped the lesson he wanted us to learn. The tale of his flinging that stone into the nose of the statue, and being chastised and sent away to another country as the outcome, was the one he used to demonstrate to us the heaviness of consequences, and the high prices we pay for poor decisions.

Obaachan flies in from Florida on a blustery November afternoon, after a series of short flights: Orlando to Atlanta, Atlanta to Dulles, Dulles to State College.

"This may be my last trip," she announces to my mother, father, brother, and me shortly after she has arrived. We are sitting around the table in my parents' kitchen. Obaachan's announcement isn't a threat or a manipulation; it's more an attempt to prepare us for the day when she will no longer be able to make the long journey north. "I'm eighty-one now, you know," she adds. When my grandmother turned eighty, she developed, almost overnight, an affection for announcing her age. She tells the clerk who gives her a senior citizen's discount at a department store, and I've even heard her introduce herself by saying, "Hello, it's nice to meet you. I'm eighty-one years old."

Obaachan has come to Pennsylvania for a two-week visit with one small carry-on suitcase. Wrapped in a wool cardigan of my mother's, she sits in the rocking chair by the woodstove, resting from the trip and looking out the window. A thin layer of snow covers the tops of things: the picnic table, the porch, the bird feeder. Black-capped chickadees and white-breasted nuthatches leap around the ledge of the feeder, pecking furiously, preparing for the long winter ahead.

"Do you think we'll see any bears?" Obaachan asks my father.

He looks up from the pot of beef stew he is stirring and smiles. Their property borders three thousand acres of state forest, so their woods are crawling with all sorts of creatures: wild turkey, whitetail deer, grouse, and, yes, black bears. My father has an ongoing battle with these black bears, mostly in the spring and fall. They steal his bird feeders and stalk around his raspberry patch. Once, he turned on the porch light late at night and discovered a bear sorting through a stash of apples on his deck. Obaachan, through nightly phone calls with my mother, has heard of these encounters, and is intrigued.

"I doubt it," my father says. "They're hibernating now. Or at least they should be." He walks over to where she is sitting and looks out. "You may see some turkeys, though. They come around sometimes. Are you comfortable there? Warm enough?"

Obaachan nods. "Oh, yes. Very comfortable."

She likes sitting by the woodstove and observing the wildlife. When my brother and I were children, she and my grandfather would watch at their window for the tall gray and red sandhill cranes. My grandparents would huddle at the bay window in their kitchen, or watch through the blinds in the living room, snap-ping photos and watching the cranes' careful path across the lawn. In his typical fashion, Ojichan decided to educate himself fully about the sandhill cranes, so that when we arrived one Christmas, he could teach us all about them. As children, we caught on to my grandparents' excitement, and we really believed that these beautiful birds, though fairly common in central Florida, were rare, and that our sightings of them were extraordinary. On her refrigerator at home, Obaachan still has a photograph that my grandfather took of these cranes.

In Florida, my grandmother walks every single morning, almost two miles, but here the days are too cold for her, and the threat of slipping on an icy patch is too much of a risk. She seems content, though, to exchange her morning walks for afternoons of reading, watching for wildlife, and dozing off with a book in her lap.

I bring her a cup of steaming hot green tea, and she takes it and wraps her hands around the cup's warm sides. Although the two of us talk on the phone some-times since I began visiting, it has been over six months since we've seen each other, and I worry that during that time she has reverted to that reticent grandmother I knew as a child—the one who sat with hands folded in the corner, only speaking in response to questions.

She turns toward me and smiles. Her glasses are large and round. Although her hair is gray, my grandmother has very few wrinkles. (*Hakujin* are more prone to wrinkles than Japanese, she and my mother have explained. I shallowly hope that I have inherited their resistance to age.) "I know what you're after, Kimi," she says. "You want to know about Ojichan. Isn't that right? I remember that last time, when we were picking grapefruit, I promised to tell you about him."

She takes a sip of tea, slurping it a little bit in the Japanese way, and I recall that my grandfather used to sip *miso* soup just like that. The steam rolls off the tea.

"The first time I spoke to your grandfather," Obaachan begins, "I was working at the mess hall. He walked right up to me and asked if I would meet him after my shift 'to talk.'" He was finely dressed, she remembers, in clothes that seemed too fashionable and too clean for the dusty confines of the camp. He wore starched khakis and a collared white shirt, and his thick, curly hair was combed off to the side, in the style many American movie stars wore in those days. He was tall for a Japanese man, and broad shouldered.

"I had noticed him before, but I'd never talked to him," Obaachan adds. She smiles. "The truth is, he was one of those people you couldn't overlook."

When Obaachan met my grandfather, he was gregarious and confident, much like the man I remember from my childhood. At Pomona, he seemed to know everyone, young and old, male and female. This sociable nature, and his tidy, stylish appearance, made my grandfather stick out. Plus, he had wavy hair, a rare characteristic for Japanese people. (This was a characteristic that he took to his grave—he died with a full head of thick, curly hair.)

Obaachan shakes her head, still impressed by these recollections. "He was the type of person who could talk to *anyone*," she says, and then she adds softly, rubbing a finger along the mug's rim, "and I was always so much the opposite."

When my grandfather first approached Obaachan at the mess hall and asked her "to talk" after work, she was mortified. Her two cousins, Uncle Kisho's stepdaughters, who lived in the same room with her family at Pomona, also worked with her. Whispering in Japanese, they giggled in the background. Obaachan's cheeks reddened, and she seemed to have lost her voice. She has admitted once that she didn't feel especially close to these cousins, and she resented their presence in this awkward moment. At last, she shook her head no, and went on with her work.

"I couldn't even manage a 'No, thank you,'" she tells me, laughing and leaning back in the rocking chair. "It was impolite of me, and you know, politeness is very important to Japanese. But I was so embarrassed I couldn't help myself."

My grandfather, however, was not easily deterred. He continued, day after day, to ask my grandmother to meet him after work. When most of the prisoners had cleared out of the mess hall, and only the workers remained, Ojichan would saunter over, lean against the counter, and make the same request, smiling and sure of himself, and without the slightest sign that he had been refused several times before.

"He kept on coming back and asking," Obaachan says, shrugging her shoulders. She herself was—and still is—perplexed by his determination. "Deep down, I was flattered and impressed. Of course, I didn't want him to know that, but finally, I said yes."

By the time my grandfather met Obaachan at the Pomona Assembly Center, he'd been living in the United States for over five years, and during those five years he had become that self-assured and outgoing man my grandmother met on a sultry afternoon in the mess hall.

Before Ojichan had left Japan, his father had made arrangements with a family friend who had moved to the United States years earlier. According to their arrangement, the friend would be waiting for my grandfather at the San Francisco docks when his ship arrived. He would then help Ojichan through the immigration process, and provide him with a home until he could find a job and support himself.

However, the family friend was not there when my grandfather's ship landed. As my grandfather stood there, searching the crowd, he pulled the letter from his shirt pocket and reread the instructions the friend had mailed his father. After two weeks of living below deck in the stuffy close quarters of third class, he was ready for fresh air, and he was also looking forward to seeing a friendly face. But no one was there. In a great horde of people, he was shuffled off the boat, and soon he found himself waiting in a long line. Even though he had studied English at his school in Japan, he did not understand a word the immigration officers spoke. He could only offer them a look of dismay and confusion. They spoke loudly and slowly, pointing to a sheet of paper, trying to signal with their hands, but my grandfather did not grasp a thing.

An old Japanese man stood nearby, arms folded, quietly observing the situation. Soon, he tossed the cigarette he was smoking to the ground, smashed it beneath his shiny shoes, and walked over to my grandfather. He placed a paternal hand on his shoulder, smiled, and asked him in Japanese if he might be of assistance. Relieved to see a welcoming face and hear his own language, my grandfather accepted the offer. The old man, fluent in both Japanese and English, helped Ojichan with the immigration procedures, translating the questions and answers. At the end, he reached out his hand and introduced himself.

"What are your plans, young man? Do you have work lined up? Family to meet?"

My grandfather scanned the crowds once more, hoping to catch sight of his father's friend. Maybe the friend had been delayed by an emergency, or perhaps he had written the wrong date on his calendar.

The old man watched my grandfather's eyes as they darted about the docks. "You are waiting for someone?" he asked.

Then again, maybe his father's friend had changed his mind.

"My father had arranged for me to meet an acquaintance of his," Ojichan told the old man at last, still looking around. "But it appears he is not here."

"Ah," the old man said, nodding his head. "It is a delicate situation," he said. He rubbed the gray bristles on his chin, surveying the crowd, and then he shrugged. "But everyone in San Francisco knows when the ships arrive," he said after a pause. "Your father's friend would be here by now if he were coming. It's a difficult time for many families right now. He has probably changed his mind and sent word to your father. You must have left before his letter arrived."

Ojichan knew that mail traveled slowly across the Pacific.

"I don't believe that we met by mere chance," the man continued. "I own a hotel right here in San Francisco, and I'm always in need of help. You will come and work for me."

Of course, in light of Ojichan's situation, this option sounded appealing, but it was really not so simple. His mind toiled through the possibilities, imagining the outcome of each scenario. If he went with the old man and his father's friend showed up, it would seem as though he had chosen to disregard the friend's generous help. It would appear disrespectful and insolent, and above all, my grandfather did not wish to further disgrace his family. He had already brought enough *haji* upon them. Yet, here he was, completely alone, unable to communicate with people, jobless, and without a friend in the entire country. He could take his chances and wait for the family acquaintance, hoping he might show up soon, or he could follow the one person who had been kind enough to assist him.

The old man picked up my grandfather's suitcase, making the decision for him. "Come along. Follow me. It's not far."

He set off on his short legs, swiftly carrying Ojichan's suitcase through the bustling, noisy streets of San Francisco. The walk to the hotel was a long one. He maneuvered his way through the multitudes of people with the grace of a dancer, while my grandfather, trying to keep up, found the noises and sights overwhelming. The honking horns of sleek Fords. The imposing businessmen in their tweed suits and fedora hats. The buttery pierogies and sweet kielbasa sizzling in the stands of street vendors.

I remember my grandfather talking about these early days in America, and how he described being on a streetcar, and seeing for the first time someone with blonde hair.

"I was sitting behind this young woman with yellow hair," he told us children. "I wanted so badly to touch it!" He wondered if it felt different from his own. In Japan, there was only one color of hair, black, so he wasn't sure the woman's yellow locks were real. Because I had grown up in Pennsylvania, and had seen people with all sorts of hair colors, this story used to strike me as strange. My father had light hair, and so did my best friend. But now, as I imagine my grandfather in those initial moments in America, I think I can understand that sensation of astonishment that he must have experienced in his first days here, and that impression that the only way to know a thing was real was to reach out and grab it.

Obaachan stands up, says that she is a little hungry, and heads to the refrigerator, where she finds one of her favorite treats: *mochi*, a sweet Japanese pastry. She places it in the toaster oven, turns the knob, shuffles over to the kitchen island, and slides herself onto one of the tall barstools. Because she is so short, her feet do not reach the floor. She settles them on the lowest rung.

"After I agreed to go on that first walk with your grandfather," she says, kicking her legs out a little and examining the pair of furry slippers my mother has bought her for the visit, "he and I started meeting more often. He would wait for me after my shifts, and we would find somewhere to talk."

The two of them would stroll around the dirt paths of the fairground, the light waning, the day still hot. Sometimes, they headed down toward the racetrack and leaned against the fence. Other days, they sat by the lagoon or circled around the old livestock barns. "We tried to make the best of the situation," Obaachan explains, folding her hands together. "We couldn't leave, so we did what we could."

It is strange for me to think about my grandparents, both in their early twenties then, getting to know each other through evening walks around a prison. And it is even stranger for me to consider the irony of their situation, for while life for the two of them remained peaceful and perhaps even promising for those months at Pomona, beyond the barbed-wire fence, the world was at war. Even in other assembly centers, there were outbreaks of violence. At Fort Sill, Oklahoma, a Los

Angeles gardener with a history of mental illness was shot to death by guards for trying to escape. At Lourdsburg, a farmer and a fisherman were also gunned down. Though the camp guards claimed they thought the two were trying to escape, it was later revealed that upon arrival at the camp, the men had been too sick after the long journey to walk from the train station to the gate, and were actually trying to make their way inside.

Furthermore, while my grandparents were prisoners at Pomona, that summer of 1942, the Nazis began gassing Jews at Auschwitz. Rommel ravaged North Africa and marched toward Cairo. And island by island, nation by nation, the little country of Japan was taking over the Pacific. They completed their capture of Burma and moved into India. In June, they invaded the Aleutian Islands. In July, New Guinea. At the height of its power, the empire of Japan controlled what was at the time the Dutch East Indies, the Philippines, French Indochina, Siam, Malaysia, Korea, and part of China. In essence, they'd taken over every piece of land from Japan to Australia.

"At times, I would almost forget," Obaachan admits, pulling her cardigan more tightly around her shoulders. "I would forget that the reason why we'd been sent away and were living this whole different life was because there was a war going on out there." But then, there were startling reminders, people and words that pulled my grandmother back into reality. At the mess hall, she picked up bits and pieces of conversations as people moved through the line. "They're going to kill us," she heard one gray-haired man whisper to another. He shifted his eyes, watching to see who else might be listening. "I've heard they will send us by train to a place where they will kill all of us. Even the women and children . . ."

The man was not alone in his fears; lots of rumors about what their fate would be made their way around the camp. The oppressive heat, the feeling of being caged, and watched, were beginning to take their toll on the residents of Pomona. As the summer progressed, my grandmother sensed that tensions had increased. At the mess hall, children grew more rambunctious, tugging at their mothers' skirts or dashing around the tables. Old folks became grumpier as they stood in line, demanding another serving of white rice or complaining that they'd been given less than the person in front of them. The prisoners were growing anxious.

In the toaster oven, the *mochi* begins to puff up to almost triple its original size, and Obaachan stands, removes it with a pair of wooden chopsticks, and places it onto a plate. When you first take *mochi* out of a refrigerator, it is small, hard, and pretty flat, similar to a cookie, but when you heat it, it grows larger, like a marshmallow over a campfire.

"Ojichan had so many stories," my grandmother continues, thinking again of my grandfather as she walks gingerly to the table. "Do you remember that about him? That he liked to tell stories?"

I nod. Many of my childhood memories consist of my sitting at my grandfather's feet, listening to him talk, watching his bushy eyebrows leap up and down.

"There was never a dull moment with him. I never felt bored," she says as she sits down at the island again. When he told her about the man at the docks, she felt as though she, too, had stood in that immigration line. When he described his first bite of a donut, she tasted its powdered sugar on her tongue. He could bring life and excitement to any tale.

"I felt that I had experienced so little," Obaachan says. "We were the same age, and yet he had *lived* so much more than I had."

While my grandfather had spent his early life in Japan and had moved as a young man to live on his own in a foreign country, my grandmother had lived a sheltered life with her parents, and had rarely left Los Angeles. While my grandfather was working at a San Francisco hotel and renting a room, my grandmother was still in the house on Pico Street, taking care of her invalid mother, dreaming of going to college one day. And while my grandmother remained close to her parents into her twenties, Ojichan never saw his family again after leaving Japan. Shortly after he had arrived in the United States, in 1938, he received a letter from his mother informing him that his father had died of stomach cancer.

"We were two very different people," Obaachan says, "from two very different worlds."

And yet there was something that drew her to him.

"I was always surprised that such an interesting person would want to be involved with someone so dull, like me," Obaachan admits, smiling a little. "At first, I didn't believe it could be true."

I consider my collection of childhood memories of my grandparents. My grandfather was always the one who talked to us and played with us. And in nearly every memory, my grandmother was standing behind him, or off to the side, her lips pressed together. While my grandfather tickled us or told stories or played hide and seek, Obaachan washed brown rice in the sink, or shelled sweet peas at the table, with the two bowls in front of her, one for the pods and one for the peas. My sense is that my grandmother always lived in my grandfather's shadow, regardless of whether or not they had visitors. He was clearly the dominant personality of the two of them. And, as my mother has told me, Ojichan was always the one in charge of their home.

My grandmother's disbelief that such a well-traveled, worldly man would take an interest in a quiet, demure young woman gets me thinking about why they *did* end up together. In some respects, she's right: my handsome, intelligent, sociable grandfather probably would have had his pick of young women, and yet he chose her. And it seems just as unlikely that Obaachan would have been attracted to an ostentatious person like my grandfather, especially because she so deeply respected her own father, who was so quiet and steady.

But perhaps my grandfather saw in Obaachan exactly what he was looking for. He knew that he could never be happy with someone vivacious and outgoing; that kind of woman would have stolen the attention from him. Instead, he needed someone who would listen to his stories, without interrupting or showing indifference, even when she had heard them a hundred times before—someone who would listen just because she loved him and knew that telling those stories gave him such joy. In other words, he needed someone like Obaachan. The fact that she had already proven herself to be a good caretaker probably didn't hurt either. My grandfather wanted children so badly, and Obaachan would have seemed like a good candidate for taking care of a family.

As for why Obaachan chose in the end to marry my grandfather—I simply ask her. The answer does not come quickly, or even directly. She sighs, thinking about it. "Well, I guess I can best explain it to you like this," she says. "In *The Forsyte Saga*, by John Galsworthy, there's a young woman who receives a marriage proposal from someone who really loves her. But she isn't sure she loves him back. When the woman asks her father what she should do, he tells her she should accept the proposal, because it is always better to be the one in a relationship who is loved more, not the one who loves more."

She pauses for a moment, pushing at the *mochi* with her chopsticks. "So what I can tell you about this is that I sensed that he loved me, even before we were married. That he really, truly loved me." She says nothing more, and I conclude that his love, his devotion, was enough for her.

By early August, Obaachan and her family knew that their time at Pomona was coming to an end. The authorities announced that within a few weeks, the prisoners would be relocated to their permanent camp. The family knew that across the country, there were ten camps, and although they had not been told where their permanent camp would be, they did understand that their departure was imminent.

My grandfather was among the first to leave. The authorities had asked for men—specifically, young, strong, and single men—to go to the permanent camp a few weeks early, and he had volunteered. No specific details were provided regarding what he and the rest of the volunteer crew would be doing; all they knew was that they would be finishing a camp somewhere.

"He saw it as a way to get out of Pomona, which he said seemed to grow smaller, hotter, and more crowded each day," Obaachan explains. "Plus it was an opportunity to make extra money."

She takes the first bite of *mochi* and tells me that it's delicious. "Would you like some? There's another in the fridge. I can cook it for you."

I tell her I don't like *mochi* very much, and she shakes her head. My brother and I are still not avid eaters of Japanese food, and Obaachan blames my mother for this. Years ago, she used to warn my mother that she needed to cook more Japanese food for us—that if we didn't eat it often enough, we wouldn't like it. Obaachan was right: we eat it, but we don't love it. The family joke is that my cousin, adopted from Korea, adores Japanese food.

"Well, just before Ojichan boarded the train to leave," Obaachan continues, "he looked at me and said that he would find me as soon as he could. We understood that we'd be going to the same place—that everyone at Pomona would be sent to one permanent camp—but that's about all we knew."

She pokes at the *mochi* with her chopstick, deflating it, and I sense how difficult it must have been for her then, saying goodbye to my grandfather. She was in the dark about so many details. Part of her feared that the rumors about being exterminated were accurate, and that my grandfather would be executed as soon as he arrived. And she felt that in those days, it was too dangerous to hope for good things—for marriage, for children, for a life with someone who cared about her. It was not so much that she didn't trust the young man she was getting to know; it was more that there had been so many changes and disappointments in the previous ten months that she was hesitant to hope for anything.

For the rest of the inmates at Pomona, the exodus began about two weeks after Ojichan left. It was a slow process: all five thousand of them could not leave at once, so the authorities divided everyone into groups and sent people away five hundred at a time. Those who remained would watch as a long line of prisoners stepped out beyond the barbed wire and marched toward the waiting trains. The armed guards, who placed themselves at every twentieth person, shouted to keep people in line. "Two feet between each person! Slow and steady!" Because small children were part of the line, everyone was ordered to walk slowly enough that the little ones could keep up.

Obaachan, standing with her father, stared as the procession of prisoners passed. Their faces showed fear, weariness, sadness, confusion. She watched the elderly struggle to keep the correct pace and worried about her own mother, who she knew would soon be making this same march. Children, just a few years old, reached for a parent's hand to hold. Some of them raised their arms to be carried.

"I wonder where it is," Obaachan said softly, hoping for some word of comfort from her father. Maybe he had heard a piece of news that he could share.

Papa shrugged. "The ten camps are in isolated locations," he said in Japanese. "Far away from coasts and major cities. Some are in the South, some in the North." He turned to look at her. "We'll find out soon enough."

"Maybe it will be another fairground, like Pomona."

He did not respond to Obaachan's speculation, but instead watched the passing line of prisoners, who left in their wake a long train of dust.

Chapter 6

THE FOLLOWING MAY, OBAACHAN FLIES TO Pennsylvania again to attend my college graduation and spend two weeks visiting my family, and she announces that while she is here, she plans to begin making a quilt. "With a pineapple pattern," she says. "For your aunt's new house in Hawaii." She'll embroider the individual squares of stiff white cotton, stitching each pattern of X's with yellow and green embroidery floss, and then she'll send the squares to the local Amish to be sewn together and quilted into the final product.

My mother, grandmother, and I have gathered in my parents' kitchen on a dreary afternoon. We've just returned from a trip to Buchanan's, the fabric store in the nearby Amish village of Belleville, and our purchases are strewn in disarray across the kitchen table, the brown bags spilling their fabric, a yellow measuring tape draping over the stacks. Even though I tend to dislike crafts, I agreed to ride along to Buchanan's in order to spend some time with my grandmother. Somehow, three hours later, it turns out I'm making a quilt of my own, a patchwork, with no embroidering required. My mother, who has always wanted a daughter who was able to sew and "be useful" in the way of household activities— she bought me a sewing machine for my graduation present—has roped me in. Now that I've spent over eighty dollars on flannels and batting, I'm regretting my decision to join them.

Obaachan and my mother, drawn to quilting and the idea of women circling up for an afternoon of gossip, are anxious to begin, and they offer their help. (Perhaps they also sense that if they don't get me started, the flannels and batting will be shoved back into their brown bag and tossed forever into a closet.) As my mother searches for some sewing supplies in her office, Obaachan stands in front of the woodstove, its warm air blowing against her back. It's unseasonably cold for this time of year and damp from all the recent rain.

My grandmother and I last talked about her imprisonment the previous fall, six months earlier, and I'm anxious to find out more about her relationship with my grandfather, along with what things were like for her at the permanent camp. So far, we haven't talked about the place where my grandparents spent over two years of their lives. But I'm nervous to ask about those years, because I still feel as though I'm prying information from her that she prefers to keep to herself, especially now that we are getting to the details about her life at Heart Mountain. That childhood conversation with my mother, when she whispered, with a hint of shame in her voice, that my grandparents had been in prison during World War II, still comes to mind sometimes. All of my questions feel like an intrusion, a ripping open of memories and years that have been sealed for a long time.

"Obaachan," I begin, peering out the window, trying to sound casual, as though we're simply continuing a conversation from an hour earlier, "Ojichan left California early, with the work crew, right? And then how long was it until you met up with him again?" I hope that returning to a detail we've already discussed—the final weeks at Pomona—might make things less awkward.

She frowns, twisting her mouth to the side, trying to remember. "Well, he left before the camp was officially open, so that was maybe in early August, maybe late July. And I think my family followed three weeks later. I don't know how long exactly, but probably fifteen or twenty days after he did. Something like that.

The days really blended into each other there. It's hard to remember."

Those final weeks at Pomona were restless for Obaachan. She had been passing the long hours in between her shifts at the mess hall with my grandfather. With him gone, there were no evening strolls down to the racetrack, no thrilling stories about Ojichan's early life in the village of Iwakuni with its lovely arched stone bridges, no dashing tales of adventures in San Francisco. For Obaachan, the hot summer days in that barbed-wire enclosure seemed endless. She wondered where my grandfather was and where she was going. There were so many questions, and in spite of her father's insistence on keeping a positive attitude, the uncertainty was beginning to bother her. Perhaps for the first time since she had met my grandfather, Obaachan felt like the prisoner she had been all along.

When her family's turn to leave Pomona finally arrived, for the second time in five months, they packed up their belongings in their five leather suitcases and the three canvas bags she and her cousins had sewn. Before they left their fairground room, her father checked to make sure each piece of luggage was labeled with their family name, and, more importantly, that their identification numbers were displayed on the white tags that hung from the handles. He stood in the doorway of that room, hands tucked into his khakis, looking at the spare walls and rough wooden floor, just as he had done before leaving the house on Pico Street earlier that year. The only things remaining in the room were the seven flimsy gray mattresses the family had dragged there on their first day. What would things be like in this new place? Would they manage to stay together, or would they be separated? And what of Mama? The future was so uncertain.

Papa turned away from the room and picked up his and Mama's belongings. By this point, the packing, unpacking, and repacking—the labeling and double-checking —had become exhausting to my grandmother and her family. The whole process of uprooting, settling, and uprooting once again seemed such an inefficient use of energy. Such a waste of life.

The two-mile march to the railroad tracks was more than Obaachan's mother was able to handle. She was ordered, along with the other handicapped and elderly passengers, to board a large Army pickup truck that would haul her to the train station. As Obaachan watched Mama pull away in that truck loaded with weary and sick passengers, she raised her hand to wave, and, for a moment, a menacing fear gripped her. What if the authorities were taking Mama to another camp? What if they sent her far away, in another direction, where no one could take care of her? Obaachan stood still, debating over whether to run after her mother. But then she remembered her father's warning about following the rules and not showing any sign of resistance. She did not dare disobey. She'd heard about what had happened to those two men at Lourdsburg, who'd been shot, and about the gardener at Fort Sill, who'd also been killed. She forced herself to look away, focusing instead on her feet, and continued marching.

After walking for over an hour, slowly, with their luggage in tow, the long column of prisoners arrived at the train station. Obaachan searched the swarm of people for her mother. Ahead, Mama was still sitting in the back of the truck with the other sick and elderly, hunched over, her hands wrapped tightly around the handle of her small suitcase. The truck was parked right next to the train tracks. Papa ran over and helped his wife to the ground, holding her at the waist.

Slowly, one by one, the group of five hundred got on the train. The old steps groaned as each person boarded. "We still didn't know where we were going," Obaachan reminds me. She shrugs. "I guess they figured we had no need to know. I mean by that point, where we were going was sort of irrelevant."

Had my grandmother and the rest of her fellow inmates known about Hitler's camps, and the long train rides hauling unsuspecting prisoners to those camps— had they seen the eerie parallels between these early

phases of their own internment and that of the European Jews—they might not have boarded that train with
such composure. Might they have resisted, hollered and
kicked, pushed at the armed men in their drab olive
uniforms, or attempted some unified revolt? Would
someone have put up a fight? When I picture myself in
this situation, I have to admit that I probably wouldn't
have led such a revolt myself. Just like my grandmother,
I would have been too scared. The stories about the
men who'd been shot, and those stern-looking soldiers
watching nearby, and their gleaming weapons—I would
have obeyed and tried to blend in, too.

When I ask my grandmother about whether she
was aware, at the time of her own imprisonment, what
happened to European Jews, she shakes her head. "We
were ignorant," she says. By the time my grandmother
was leaving Pomona, Hitler had been shipping prisoners
to concentration camps since 1941, and he'd been gassing them for months, but the Allies did not discover
those camps until months later, in December of 1942.
Obaachan sighs. "In a strange sense, I guess our ignorance protected us."

As Obaachan and her family settled into their seats,
armed guards arrived to pace the aisles. The air in
that train, crammed with its five hundred passengers,
quickly grew thick and stifling. Outside, the August

temperatures were unrelenting, and the odor of five hundred people who'd just walked two miles in those temperatures became nauseating. Finally, with a tired sigh, the train began to ease forward.

In those initial hours on the train, the excitement of leaving behind the crowded room at Pomona gave Obaachan a renewed sense of hope. She tried to guess where they were headed, and what the new apartment would be like. Maybe this permanent camp wouldn't be so bad, she told herself. Maybe Papa would have a garden again, a small one, with irises and tulips, and maybe there would be a front porch where Mama could sit in the afternoons.

"At first, the trip was sort of a thrill," Obaachan says. "Aside from my trip to Japan as a little girl, I'd basically never left Los Angeles. So this was almost like going to another country for me. We went through parts of the United States that I'd never seen before, parts I thought I'd never see."

My grandmother watched as the Arizona desert raced by, its sand and rocks a blur at the window. She saw the landscape slowly shifting to where outcroppings of rock jutted up from the ground, sharp and red, imposing and towerlike. "I didn't see as much of those states as you might think. Through some of the towns, they made us close the blinds," Obaachan explains. On previous train trips, the residents of these towns, provoked by the sight of so many Japanese, had hurled rocks at the windows of the train and hollered insults. The officials decided it was best to avoid such outbursts by hiding the prisoners from the angry crowds outside.

After several hours, the sun, now sinking behind them, grew orange and began to cast long shadows, and those passengers who were riding backward squinted and shaded their eyes. At last, night began to overtake them. Obaachan watched as the desert's rocky hills formed into outlines at the window, and then faded into complete darkness. Some passengers were able to sleep, exhausted from the packing, marching, and sitting, but many remained wide awake. Obaachan's back was badly cramped from sitting for so many hours without moving, and she struggled to get comfortable. These days, as a woman in her eighties, she seems able to fall asleep just about anywhere, and she often nods off on long car rides, or even as she sits at her desk reading, but when she was young, she had trouble sleeping in an upright position. To her left, in the aisle seat, her mother slept, leaning against her side. Obaachan wanted to stretch her back and legs, but since she didn't want to wake Mama, she tried not to think about the pinching pain in her back and forced herself to be as still as possible.

She thought instead about that young man she'd said goodbye to three weeks earlier: his wavy black hair, parted and combed carefully to the side; his clean, starched button-downs; and his wide, easy smile. She imagined him waiting for her at the train station. Even though my grandmother had not made up her mind about him just yet, she hoped that he hadn't lost interest in her. After three weeks without contact, Obaachan feared that with his sociable nature and his dislike of being alone, he might have moved on to someone prettier or more interesting. She shifted her thoughts from my grandfather to other things. The feel of Papa's fresh bamboo shoots in her palm. Sunday afternoons at the beach where the sand was so hot it stung her feet. Sitting around a campfire and roasting hot dogs on sticks. Eating fresh watermelon on the front porch with Jack and Papa, the sweet, pink juice trickling down her chin. Eventually, late into the night, she drifted off.

By early morning, the children were growing restless on that train. They squirmed in their mothers' laps and kicked at the backs of the seats in front of them. Obaachan felt sorry for them, for their cramped muscles, hunger, boredom, and exasperation. The sensation of being trapped with nowhere to go. Some children cried or whimpered, and when one would begin, often another child would hear it and begin crying as well. It reminded her of how sometimes the dogs in her neighborhood back in Los Angeles would join each other in barking, how a cacophony of howls would start from a single yelp.

"I remember stopping once, in Albuquerque," Obaachan says. "I think that was the only time." It seems likely that the family switched trains there, since the Atchison, Topeka, and Santa Fe line came to an end in Albuquerque. For about fifteen minutes, all the prisoners were permitted to exit the train and walk around the platform of the station. Obaachan's father helped Mama step from the train, and he looped elbows with her to help her walk. Huddled together, with Mama resting against Papa's shoulder, the two of them took tiny steps along the tracks. The guards, intimidating in their stiff uniforms and shiny, knee-high boots, eyed the prisoners warily, gripping their machine guns and circling around.

On the fourth day of the trip, Obaachan finally heard the brakes and felt the train begin to slow. The passengers whispered and stretched to see out the windows.

"Remain in your seats," warned the guards. "Stay seated."

A few rebels, unable to resist the urge to get a look at their new home, lifted the blinds to see out.

"What's out there? Tell us what you see!" a young man shouted.

Those who had lifted the blinds offered descriptions: There's a high barbed-wire fence, and towers, just like Pomona.

I see one mountain, not too far away.

No trees! I see no trees at all! And it's very rocky, like a desert.

The train groaned and then lurched to a stop.

"Attention!"

Eager for details and instructions, the crowd grew quiet.

A uniformed *hakujin* man stood outside the train, holding a megaphone.

"He said that we should consider the place our home until the War Authority told us otherwise," Obaachan says. The prisoners were ordered to stay together with their families, and to exit the train in an orderly fashion. The registration, which would go by number and not family name, would take some time, and they would need to be patient.

"Excuse me, sir," an older gentleman said to a guard who stood beside him. "Where are we?"

The guard refused to look at the man and seemed annoyed with the question. "Wyoming," he said, stepping off the train, and then he called over his shoulder, "Heart Mountain."

Heart Mountain earned its name from a nearby rocky hill jutting up from the stark Wyoming plain that, from an aerial view, formed the shape of a heart. It was located on a forty-six-thousand-acre reserve, but the barbed-wire enclosure where my grandparents and their fellow prisoners actually lived was only a square mile in size. The prison site had been selected because it met three specifications. First, the camp had to be far enough away from any towns to avoid conflict with the local *hakujin*, who were wary about the arrival of thousands of dangerous "Japs" in their territory. Located thirteen miles from Cody and twelve miles from Powell, in the northwest corner of Wyoming, Heart Mountain was surrounded by enough desert to be considered safe. Secondly, a water source capable of sustaining ten thousand people had to be available: the nearby Shoshone River met this requirement. And lastly, an economical means of getting supplies in and out of the camp was necessary. To meet this demand, the Vocation Railroad guaranteed cheap transportation of supplies.

Back in April, when the government was still in its early stages of planning for permanent relocation centers, the governor, Nels Smith, who knew there was talk of building a camp in Wyoming, had announced that if the Japanese were permitted in *his* state, they would "be hanging from every tree." While some other Wyoming politicians voiced similar concerns, for the most part, residents were not opposed to the construction of the Heart Mountain camp. Their area, like the rest of the country, had suffered through the hardships of the Great Depression, and many of the locals saw the camp as a potential reprieve, a source of employment and an opportunity to boost the dragging economy. Still, even if people realized the economic benefits, interactions between Japanese prisoners and *hakujin* locals would have been tense.

After all, the summer of 1942 had been especially bloody in the Pacific. Throughout the slow, sweltering month of August, the United States and Japan struggled in battle after battle. On the night of August 8, the Allies suffered an agonizing defeat: Japan sank three American heavy cruisers, an Australian cruiser, and a US destroyer, killing over fifteen hundred Allied crewmen. On August 17, the Americans attacked Makin Atoll in the Gilbert Islands, and on August 21, they repulsed the first major Japanese ground attack on Guadalcanal. In another Allied victory on August 24, they defeated the Japanese in the Battle of the Eastern Solomons. On August 29, the Red Cross announced that Japan was refusing to grant safe passage of ships containing supplies for American POWs.

Knowing these details about the war, especially that final one, that Japan had prevented supplies from being shipped to American prisoners, I can imagine the unease that Wyoming residents would have felt as thousands of Japanese prisoners poured into their state. I remember something Ojichan told my brother and me as children, and I wonder if he'd adopted the mind-set during the war. In his serious, emphatic way, he urged us, as though his message held grave importance, to remember that we were always representatives of our race when we interacted with others.

"You might be the only Japanese a person ever meets," he insisted, "and that person will judge the entire race based on how *you* act. It might not seem fair, but it's true."

As a child, I found this concept alarming. On the one hand, I didn't fully believe my grandfather—certainly people were not so foolish as to make assumptions about an entire race of people based on one person's behavior, let alone a child's—and yet on the other hand, my mother, brother, and I probably *were* the only Japanese people most of the residents in our tiny Pennsylvania town ever met. Located in the Alleghenies, just south of the middle of the state, our county was predominantly comprised of white folks whose families had lived in Pennsylvania for decades or even centuries. (My father's *hakujin* family fell into the latter category; his Irish ancestors had arrived in the eighteenth century.) A handful of minorities lived in the area, and as far as I knew, my mom, brother, and I were the only Japanese people. So I think it was with a blend of resistance and resignation that I accepted my grandfather's advice, and tried my best to be on good behavior, at least some of the time.

The teapot my mother put on the stove begins to sputter and hiss, and Obaachan stands up, takes a cup from the cupboard, and gingerly pours the steaming water. "This part of my memory—the whole arrival—is not good, Kimi. I just can't remember much of it." She dips the teabag into the mug, bobs it up and down, studies the way the color slowly bleeds into the water. "I don't remember getting off the train, the weather, or anything. I only remember that I was with my parents."

She knows, however, that the arrival was hectic and stressful. After four days on that train, everyone was anxious to get off and to be assigned their new room. Some people, like my grandmother, would have been searching the crowd for a familiar face, hoping to see a person they'd said goodbye to weeks earlier. Others would have been focused solely on the task of gathering their luggage and getting into the registration line as quickly as possible. Remembering that those who'd been last to register at Pomona had been given straw mattresses, no one wanted to waste time. Obaachan huddled with her mother, holding onto Mama's arm, next to a nearby barrack while her father searched the heap of suitcases that had been dumped beside the train. He grabbed the tags and checked the numbers. Slowly, piece by piece, he gathered up their bags and suitcases.

"At this point, Papa and Uncle Kisho had decided that our two families could live in separate quarters. We knew this was the permanent camp. There was no need for the seven of us to go on living in a single room," Obaachan explains, taking a sip of tea and returning to the kitchen table. "I mean, we all got along, but by that point, we were looking forward to not being so crammed."

I ask her if she remembers when my grandfather found her, or where, and she frowns and shakes her head.

"Did he meet you at the gate? Or did he come to your family's room?" I press, hoping to remind her. But the questions aren't helpful. Obaachan's still squinting, trying to recall the details. She shakes her head. "Maybe because he'd been there for awhile, he knew how to find out if a family had been registered, and where they were living. Maybe we just ran into each other. Like I said, this part is a blur."

I realize I'd been hoping for some romantic memory of their meeting up again, something Hollywood. I wanted to hear that my grandfather had been waiting for her, that he was by the gate, waving, smiling, trying to get her attention. Or maybe that the morning after they'd arrived, he'd shown up on the front porch, looking sharp in his khaki slacks and starched shirt, and maybe with some sort of small gift. A flower he'd picked, perhaps, or an extra treat from the mess hall. But whatever the turn of events might have been, my grandmother can't remember a thing. Or doesn't want to.

"Sorry," Obaachan says.

I can't tell if she is apologizing for not being able to remember, or if she's sorry she's not ready to relive this part of the experience yet, or if she feels that the story itself is disappointing me. And I don't know how to respond to this apology. I glance at my mother, who is smoothing out a large folded piece of flannel for my quilt, trying to line up the edges. She has been listening quietly to this conversation, taking in each and every detail. Hearing her mother talk about the camp is a rare experience for her—it is something her parents never spoke of in their house in New Jersey, and something she never asked about.

Obaachan runs her hand over a piece of fabric and then stands up. "I need to rest now," she says. "I'm going to sit on the rocker and watch the birds. I'm eighty-two and I don't have the stamina that I used to." She says the word "stamina" carefully, spitting out each syllable, as she often does when she uses longer words. Even though my grandmother has spoken only English for decades now, she still has an accent, more because of her intonation than her pronunciation, and noticeable only at times. She shuffles over to the window by the woodstove.

As I watch her settle into the rocking chair and begin to ease back and forth, her head high, her eyes focused on the bird feeder, her slippers tapping lightly on the carpet, I sense that in her mind she is elsewhere right now, far away, in some cold and snowy place.

Chapter 7

Months after Obaachan's visit, a few days before Christmas, my mother calls me at my apartment in State College, Pennsylvania. Her voice is labored and anxious. I sense bad news. She breathes deeply into the phone and says it: Obaachan has just been diagnosed with breast cancer. "The right side," my mother continues. She pauses, sorting through the words. "They say it's not very big. That she probably won't need chemo because they might be able to get rid of it with surgery and targeted radiation. She's scheduled for early next month. You should call her."

I agonize over making that phone call to my grandmother. I've never been good at sensing how such conversations should go. Is it better to begin the exchange with an apology—I'm sorry to hear your bad news—or is it best to talk about other things and then, after a few moments of small talk, shift with caution to the topic of the diagnosis? I decide to take the latter route, thinking I might help my grandmother feel "normal" by not making her cancer the first thing I mention. The plan fails. As I fumble through questions about the weather in Florida and what she plans on cooking for New Year's, she interrupts and says, in that matter-of-fact way of hers, "I'm sure by now your mother has told you about my cancer." She doesn't even struggle with that last word when she says it, doesn't pause anywhere in the sentence.

Like all cancer diagnoses, my grandmother's is a shock. Even though I understand that attention to one's health doesn't entirely protect a person from getting cancer, I think of Obaachan's scrupulous attention to her health. She exercises daily on her walks around the neighborhood; she eats a balanced, varied diet (she actually counts out the number of peanuts in the suggested serving size) and grows her own fruit; and she has enjoyed good health her whole life.

Despite the shock, Obaachan faces the diagnosis with resolve and her characteristic Japanese mentality of *shikataganai*. Whatever happens, happens. You cannot change your fate, so don't bother feeling sorry for yourself. Obaachan schedules the surgery and preop appointments, makes travel arrangements with my aunt to spend two days in Tampa for the lumpectomy, and eventually begins a regimen with a physical therapist to strengthen the chest and shoulder tissues. By March, when I'm to make my annual visit to Florida, she has recovered from the surgery, and her oncologist clears her to begin radiation.

I'm near the end of my first year of teaching high school English, and I'm drained from the long evening hours of lesson plans and worksheets. Obaachan and I have not seen each other since the previous May, when she came to Pennsylvania for my college graduation, and I look forward to a visit, where we can have some uninterrupted time to ourselves. On my first trip to Florida, three years earlier, I'd been nervous about spending a whole week with this woman I hardly knew. Since she'd always been so quiet during my childhood visits with her, I'd assumed she was antisocial. I'm ashamed to admit that, as a teenager, I'd also wondered if she didn't like me. Now, we talk on the phone sometimes, about every other week, so I am not as nervous as I was in our early meetings.

The center where Obaachan goes for radiation is twenty minutes north of her home, a bit far for a daily drive, but better than heading all the way back to Tampa, where she had her surgery. Each morning of my week in Florida, the two of us leave the house by eight thirty to make sure she gets there for her nine o'clock appointment. The first time, as we drive out of her

neighborhood and make our way to I-95, she explains
that the radiation doesn't take long, that I can sit in the
waiting room while she changes and heads back to her
appointment. She has been going for two weeks now,
alone. So far, she has few side effects: she seems a little
more tired, a little weaker, but that's it.

"Did you know that men can get breast cancer?"
Obaachan asks as we pull onto the highway. She is seated
beside me, on the passenger side. Whenever she has the
opportunity to ride, rather than drive, she takes it. In her
quiet neighborhood, most people obey the twenty-five-
miles-per-hour speed limit, and the roads are wide and
open. Once you leave the immediate area, though, the
traffic is heavy, the drivers are aggressive, and the various
turn lanes can be overwhelming. Plus, my grandmother
explained yesterday, people in Florida don't like to see old
folks driving, and she doesn't like to make anyone angry.
(She has been reading editorials and letters to the editor
about this subject in her local paper recently.)

Obaachan continues talking about men and breast
cancer. "I met a man at the breast-care center in Tampa,
and when I asked him if he was waiting for his wife, he
told me that he was a *patient*." She chuckles, shaking her
head in disbelief. "At first I thought he was making a
joke." I picture my grandmother trying to humor this
man in the waiting room of a hospital as he attempted
an awkward joke. A breast-cancer patient herself, she

certainly wouldn't have found him amusing, but she wouldn't be rude, either. "Then he went on to explain to me the whole procedure of how they found the lump, and what he had to do. And then I realized he was serious. I had no idea it could happen to a man."

We drive in silence for a few minutes, and I struggle with what to say. I want to tell my grandmother that I'm sorry she has to deal with such a thing. And I want to say that it seems unfair, somehow, that she was diagnosed with this disease, after all the setbacks—the displacements and illnesses and loss—she has already faced. I wonder if she finds herself thinking of Ojichan, who passed away eight years earlier, of pulmonary fibrosis. Or if she remembers her mother's long struggle of living with an irregular heartbeat, the ups and downs of having a debilitating illness in the internment camp. I sense, however, that Obaachan doesn't want my sympathy, nor does she want me to think too much about the parallels between her cancer and anyone else's problems. In her mind, cancer is just another card life has dealt her, and my desire to overanalyze it is just another sign that I fail to handle things with the ease and tenacity that a Japanese person should.

Obaachan turns down the radio so that we can talk. Conversations tend to be difficult in the car, especially when she is in the passenger seat, with her good ear to the window. "I know you want to know more," she begins. "About Heart Mountain, I mean. That's where Ojichan and I were for most of the war. We were there for . . ." Her voice trails off. She is trying to remember. "We got there in August of 1942, and we left in the summer of 1945, right before Victory in Japan Day. So just under three years."

By the time she arrived in Wyoming, my grandmother had technically been a prisoner of the US government for five months, but she recognized that this new phase was different. "I think before, when we were at Pomona, it didn't hit me that this was a long-term situation," Obaachan says, adjusting the air vents on the passenger side of the car. "We were so close to LA. We were still in California, our home state, plus we knew all along it was only temporary. And then when I got to Heart Mountain, I think I realized we were going to be there for a long time. Maybe for years, maybe forever." The WRA made no promises regarding the future of the Japanese who'd been evacuated from the West Coast. My grandmother and her family only hoped that they would be freed when the war ended.

That August evening when Obaachan arrived at Heart Mountain, she and her family gathered their belongings and registered with the officials, then made their way through the dirt streets and rows of barracks.

It was easy to get turned around in that collection of identical buildings: all of them had low roofs and black tar paper covering the walls. In all, there were thirty blocks, each of which consisted of somewhere between twelve and fourteen housing barracks. My grandmother and her parents were in Block 17.

Uncle Kisho, his wife, and his two stepdaughters registered separately, and went to find their own assigned place, a few blocks away. Papa carried both his and Mama's bags, while Obaachan helped her mother up the front steps. The rickety porch creaked as they climbed the stairs and walked toward the entrance of their room. Papa opened the wooden door, and the three of them stepped into their new home.

Inside, it was sparse and dark. The floors were made of long, rough-cut boards, and there was no insulation whatsoever. In fact, no interior walls had been built, so the studs and plywood were visible. A small black coal stove stood in one corner, and three cots with thin pinstriped mattresses were the only furniture. A plain light hung from the ceiling, tossing a faint yellow glow upon the room. On one side, a small window let in the last red rays of the setting sun.

Each 20-foot-by-120-foot housing barrack consisted of six apartments. Generally, the two on either end were reserved for couples. They were smaller and offered a little more privacy. The next two apartments were slightly larger and often housed six people or so. Sometimes large families lived in these, but in many cases, groups of single people who had come to Heart Mountain without any family members would stay in them. Ojichan lived in such a room. My grandmother and her parents were assigned to live in one of the two middle apartments, in a 320-square-foot space.

Obaachan and I continue along I-95, in the slower traffic of the right lane because I am unaccustomed to the seventy-miles-per-hour speed limits of Central Florida. Even though I've set the cruise control to this speed, it seems I'm moving way too slowly for the rest of the drivers: SUVs with tinted windows and shiny convertibles race past us. Obaachan slides her index finger along the handle of her purse. She turns to face me.

"The apartment was small, but remember, Kimi, things weren't like they are now. Our standard of living was much different. Now, people have so many belongings, so much space. I'd grown up in the Great Depression." She shrugs. "Sure, there was no paint on the walls, no furniture besides the cots. But it was not that disappointing. You probably don't understand."

My own apartment, back in Pennsylvania, was renovated just before my roommate and I signed the lease, so we moved into a place with all brand-new appliances, new windows, fresh paint, and shiny wooden floors. There's a bathroom, living room, kitchen, two bedrooms, and a giant attic spanning the length of the house for storage—all for just two of us. At this point in my life, I can't imagine leaving this spacious apartment and moving into a small room with my mother and father. We get along well, but three of us in such a small space would be pretty awful.

Obaachan continues. "That first night, we could hear people settling in all around us." She frowns. "That was the thing about those apartments. You had absolutely no privacy. You could hear *everything*." The walls that divided one apartment from the next did not reach the ceiling, so there was a foot of open space at the top of each divider. On one side, Obaachan heard a din of male voices, men introducing themselves to one another. She later learned that her family lived next to one of Heart Mountain's bachelor quarters. On the other side, a mother hushed the questions of a child, who asked why the floor was so rough, and whether it was going to get warmer in their room, and when they were allowed to eat dinner. Somewhere, not right next door but maybe a few apartments away, a baby was crying.

"We had the bachelors to the left, and then on the other side, we had a family of four," Obaachan says as we pass another exit. "A younger couple with two small children. They were maybe in their late twenties or early thirties. It was sort of strange with them, though, because the husband would go away on the work crews to pick beets in Montana, and whenever he was gone, and the children were at school, this other man would come to the apartment, and spend all afternoon in there with the wife." Obaachan wrinkles her face in disapproval.

"Maybe he was her tutor," I say, half teasing, half testing to see how she will react. "Maybe she was trying to learn English, or math or something."

"Well, maybe, but he never came by when the husband was around," she says sharply. "So it was a little suspicious."

I ask her if she or anyone else ever said anything about it to the husband, and she shakes her head. "It wasn't our business. Japanese don't get involved with other people's personal affairs. That's not the way we do things." She points to the next exit, and I flip on the turn signal. "This is where you get off," she says. "Turn left off the ramp, and it's the brown building on your right. See, there's the sign."

We pull into the parking lot of the radiation center and climb out of the car. As we walk through the front door of the building, Obaachan transforms into her more businesslike, private self—into that guarded, mysterious woman I knew as a child. "You have to wait here," she says, ushering me into a small room with stacks of magazines and a game of Scrabble on the center table. A middle-aged man sits in the corner, reading *Sports Illustrated*. Obaachan informs me she'll come out when she's finished. She doesn't want me going beyond that waiting room, and into the small changing stall where she will slip out of her clothes and drape a thin hospital gown over her shoulders.

She walks away, down the dark hallway, and leaves me standing alone in the center of the room. I pick up a copy of *The Atlantic* and settle into a red stiff-backed chair in the corner. But as I leaf through the color spreads I worry about her. Her prognosis is encouraging—the doctors think that she's now clear—and from what I can tell she seems to be feeling well. And yet I know enough about cancer to understand that it is resilient and deceptive, and that having surgery and radiation or even chemotherapy doesn't guarantee you'll survive. In this moment, in the cool, dark waiting room of that office, I wish I could summon that *shikataganai* way of thinking—that ability to surrender to whatever fate lies ahead—but I can't. I worry about what will happen to her, worry about something I cannot control.

Twenty minutes later, Obaachan emerges from her radiation appointment, her white cardigan wrapped around her shoulders, her purse tucked beneath her arm. She stands in the doorway, more relaxed now, smiling. "All done," she says. "It's pretty fast, right? In and out."

I grab my handbag and check the page I'm on in the story in *The Atlantic*, so that I can pick up there the following morning, when we return for another round of radiation. Obaachan glances at my magazine and asks me if I read any of the book reviews. She's always looking for her next book. She rarely buys books these days—aside from the annual used-book sale the Friends of the Library hosts, where she usually picks up a handful of one-dollar paperbacks—and she only reads what she can borrow from the library, which requires planning ahead. If the book she wants isn't there, she orders it through interlibrary loan, but in the meantime, she has to find something else to read. I tell her I was reading a short story, but that I'll check the reviews tomorrow.

The two of us walk outside into the bright Florida morning and climb back into Obaachan's car. Less than an hour has passed since we left the house, but the day has warmed significantly. I push the buttons to open the windows and let the car cool. Even in March, the seventy-degree weather can feel hot, especially when you're visiting from the Northeast and accustomed to temperatures in the thirties. I shield my eyes and tell Obaachan how nice it is to escape the Pennsylvania winter. We pull out of the parking lot and head back to the highway.

"You get used to certain climates," Obaachan says. "Your body settles into a place, I think. Like for us, when we got to Heart Mountain, it was already cold. We'd just come from Southern California. I didn't even own a winter coat." Very few of the prisoners did. After a few months, the War Authority realized this was a problem and distributed navy peacoats, identical ones, to each person. Mama and Aunt Maki had the nice coats with fur collars their husbands had purchased just before leaving Los Angeles, but they were among a select few. Most of the prisoners had no choice but to wear the peacoats they were given. In the harsh Wyoming winters, they would not have been sufficient.

In fact, for my grandmother, the weather was one of the most difficult adjustments. She was used to sunshine and warmth, the sounds of crying seagulls and the crashing of the ocean; the salty, pungent scent of the beach. In Wyoming, there was nothing but dirt and sagebrush, which tumbled aimlessly along the streets. Long, melancholy plains that ached with sadness. There, the snow arrived in September, and once it began, storm after storm followed, and the snow never had the chance to melt. It piled higher as the winter progressed, and the heaps workers shoveled to the sides of the paths and along the buildings only grew larger.

At night, the wind whistled through the long rows of barracks and thrashed against the thin tar-paper walls. "The sound was awful," Obaachan says, wrinkling her nose. "It was like a woman screaming. And the wind, it kicked up the sand and pelted your face." Papa stuffed rags under the door to block out the dirt because it would blow beneath the wide crack and spread itself all over their belongings. These rags helped to a degree, but it seemed that no matter how many of them were used or how often the family swept, a thin layer of dust covered the floors. They'd find grains of sand in their bed sheets and in the folds of their clothing, too.

"In the winter, you avoided being outdoors whenever possible. But you could only stay in that room for so long. I mean, we had to eat and use the restrooms, wash our clothes, bathe." While the mess hall was not too far away, the bathroom was almost a block from their room. Obaachan fiddles with the handle of her purse. "My mother—it was tough on her. She couldn't walk that far, not in that kind of weather, with all the snow and cold." Instead, Obaachan's mother used a small metal chamber pot in the room. Each morning Papa would haul it to the men's restroom and clean it out for her.

The lack of privacy—in Obaachan's mother having to use the chamber pot with her husband and daughter there in the room, and her father having to take it to a public place and wash it—was a source of *haji* for all three. "We Japanese are very private people," Obaachan explains. Even growing up, she and her sister, who shared a bedroom on Pico Street, would avert their eyes to avoid seeing each other as they dressed or undressed. And Obaachan understood that she was not allowed to snoop and meddle in her siblings' affairs, or play with their toys without permission. I am sure that in recent months, all the undressing and exposing herself to strange doctors and nurses has been quite jarring to her, no matter how many times she has done it.

Pausing for a moment, Obaachan points to the entrance ramp I need to take to get back on the interstate. "When we were at Heart Mountain, though, our privacy was taken from us."

The public restrooms were set up in such a way that privacy was impossible. Partitions separated one toilet from the next, but there were no doors. The showers were public as well, with no curtains or individual stalls. "We undressed and then had to walk what seemed like an endless distance to the shower, naked. Down a long hallway. Many women tried holding a washcloth over—you know, to cover themselves, and try to hold on to some sense of dignity." Obaachan shivers a bit, still disgusted by the experience, still a little ashamed of having been forced to parade herself in front of so many strangers during those years at Heart Mountain.

"Once, I was in the shower at the same time as another young woman. There were always eight or ten of us in at a time. The girl was probably close to me in age, and her back was covered with a blanket of dark hair." (Most Japanese people lack visible body hair, even men, so this sight would have been shocking for my grandmother.) "I'd never seen anything like it, and something about it made me want to stare, but I forced myself to look away instead." She frowns. She was ashamed of looking at the young woman. She was ashamed for her. For everyone.

Using the toilet was even more humiliating than showering. Obaachan hated sitting on that cold porcelain rim, trying not to be nervous as other women passed by, their shampoo and towels in hand, or stood gossiping at the sinks. Whenever possible, she would try to get the toilet farthest from the sinks and showers, where the distance made things feel a little more private. With the starchy diet of bread, white rice, hot dogs, and canned beans, many of the prisoners suffered from diarrhea, which made the whole matter of using the toilet even more unpleasant. Eventually, because so many people complained, the officials added doors to the toilet stalls. I can't help wondering, though, why no doors were installed in the first place. Was there not enough time? Or was the dehumanizing element of having no privacy intentional—to drive home the point that the prisoners were, in the eyes of the law, now second-class citizens?

During the winter, the long walk outside from the bathroom to her apartment was an agonizing trek after a shower. Although the water was always decently hot, Obaachan knew that the trip home would be painful. Stepping out into the frigid, gusty weather promptly turned her hair into clumps of icicles. She traveled as swiftly as possible, clutching her bottle of shampoo, tucking her chin into her coat. "You had to walk carefully, though," she says. "The shoveled paths could be icy." That first winter at Heart Mountain, one of the coldest on record in the state of Wyoming, temperatures dipped to thirty degrees below zero.

Obaachan and I drive in silence for a few moments, through a rare undeveloped patch of central Florida, where the side of the road is covered in thick, brushy undergrowth, and a herd of brawny black cattle graze, their hides nappy and caked with mud. I sense that my grandmother is through with talking about the shameful elements of the restrooms at Heart Mountain for now, so I attempt to give her something else to talk about. "What did you and Ojichan do? I mean for fun. I know at Pomona, you mostly walked around the fairgrounds, but what about at Heart Mountain? With the weather, I'm guessing you had to find other things to do."

Obaachan presses her lips together, concentrating. "Well, we found ways to kill time, I guess. They had different shows and things, like a show with different *ikebana*, or flower arrangements. And sometimes they had *kabuki* performances, you know, Japanese theatre. We went to those, I guess, and then sometimes, he would come to our apartment and talk, but only if my parents were there." She pauses. "But mostly we saw a lot of movies." *Casablanca. For Whom the Bell Tolls. Meet Me in St. Louis.* "I saw every single one they showed there." She grins sheepishly, turning to look at me. "I told you I've always liked movies," she says.

My grandmother wasn't the only one who looked to movies as a source of diversion. In the three years that Heart Mountain remained open, they were the most popular form of entertainment for the prisoners, with a total attendance of 600,908. At first, the authorities showed these movies in the mess halls, a few hours after the evening meal. One showing would begin at seven, and then, maybe an hour into the film, when the first reel ran out, they would load the second reel, and someone would carry the first reel to a different mess hall, where another showing would begin for a second audience. Then, on October 24, 1942, two "theatres" officially opened, "The Dawn" and "The Pagoda." Tickets were ten cents apiece, but my grandmother never paid to see a single film.

Before the theatres opened, the authorities had announced a contest to see which prisoner could come up with the best name for each one. Obaachan's mother submitted the name "The Dawn" and won herself a lifetime pass to see as many movies as she wanted. Of course, as an invalid, Mama could not use the pass, so she asked for permission to give it to her daughter, and the authorities agreed to the transfer. Thanks to Mama's inventive mind, my grandparents were able to enjoy many "dates" for half the cost.

"What did your parents think of Ojichan?" I feel sure that my own father would have disapproved of the bragging, the expensive clothing, and the ostentatious personality—but I don't mention this.

"They liked him," Obaachan says, as though she's surprised I would need to ask. "First of all, he spoke Japanese, so they liked that. Remember, my parents didn't speak English. And as I've said, your grandfather was the type of person who could talk with anyone. So they approved, if that's what you mean. We were married by December, you know, four months after we got to Heart Mountain. December 12. My mother said it was a good omen, that date."

From the beginning of their relationship, my grandfather had made clear to Obaachan his intentions: he wanted to get married and have a family, and he planned to do it soon. I imagine that in those final months of 1942, as the war pressed on and their life at Heart Mountain seemed to feel more and more permanent, Ojichan would have done his best to woo my grandmother, to secure her as his wife. He would've continued working to impress her with fabulous stories from his youth—and the wealth of worldly wisdom he'd gained from that youth. Sixty years after first hearing these tales, Obaachan still recalls them, sometimes more vividly than stories of her own. My grandfather would be pleased, I think, to know that his attempts to gain Obaachan's interest made a lasting impression. With his colorful personality and his desire, even as a man in his seventies, to be the focus of a crowd's attention, he would be happy to know that his efforts weren't wasted.

"Did I ever tell you about the millionaire I worked for in San Francisco?" Ojichan asked one evening, when they were walking home from a movie. Without waiting for a response, he continued. "I was a houseboy. I ran errands, helped the gardener. I spent a lot of time with the chef, doing prep work, washing dishes, cooking." The family owned a vineyard, and even during the Depression, they had enough money for servants. Each Monday morning, the lady of the house would make up a menu with the chef, tell him what she wanted to eat that week, and the chef would go to the market, or send Ojichan, and they'd make whatever the woman had requested.

Obaachan had never met a millionaire, let alone worked for and lived on the property of one, and my grandfather's story caught her attention. She had eaten in a restaurant only a handful of times, and that alone was a big deal to her. Back in Los Angeles, even though her family had never gone hungry, her mother planned their meals around what her father was able to bring home from his job at the produce market. The idea of deciding what you felt like eating, without giving a thought to the cost, and then having a person whose primary job was to buy your food and prepare it for you, was almost beyond her ability to imagine.

"The food was wonderful," my grandfather said. "Delicious, elegant. I wish you could have seen the way they set up the table each night. Starched white linens, tall candlesticks with real silver holders, fine English china. I only hope I can live like that someday—that the two of us can, together—without having to think about money." Ojichan chuckled and kicked at a heap of snow, and the two continued on their way.

I wonder if my grandfather's taste for fine things— and his attraction to the power those fine things implied—began when he was working as a houseboy for that family. What I do know is that by the time he met my grandmother in 1942, his affection for fashionable clothing, expensive whiskey, and well-made shoes was already strong. In photographs taken at Heart Mountain, my grandfather is always dressed as though he's heading to an afternoon at the races, or a polo match, or some high-society event. His thick hair is combed to the side, his shirt is stiff and tucked in, and his khakis show a neat crease down the middle of the leg. How he managed to look so dapper in the dust-laden bachelor barracks remains an eternal mystery.

Obaachan admits she was swept away by my grandfather's good looks and fancy clothes. She was inspired, too, by the big dreams he had for himself, for his ambition and his belief that anything at all was possible in America, despite their situation. Because of his fondness for nice things, his plans for the future often involved making a lot of money. He was always coming up with schemes to make it big: creating new inventions that would fill some niche, or starting a shipping company. In San Francisco, he'd heard countless stories of people striking it rich, and he seemed convinced, even in the somber confines of the internment camp, that America was a land without limits, that this time of trouble would pass.

I slow the car and turn into Obaachan's neighborhood. At the half-acre lake near the entrance to her development, I pull over so that we can take a quick look at the water. A blue heron spots us, spreads its wide wings, and flies off. Yesterday, on our way to the supermarket, we saw a young alligator in this pond, and we're hoping to find it again. The alligator's small enough—maybe three feet in length—to be interesting but not frightening.

"There," Obaachan says, pointing. "Is that it?" She covers a yawn with her hand. Usually, she doesn't grow tired until late afternoon, but radiation treatments, notorious for their enervating effect, make her sleepy, even before lunch.

I tell her I think what she sees is just a clump of leaves near the pond's drain. We pull away slowly, still looking for it. Obaachan reaches for the garage door opener, which is tucked in the middle console.

"It didn't take your grandfather long to start talking about marriage," she says. "In fact, it became his primary topic of conversation." She was willing to wait. Something deep inside of her was not yet ready to take that step. "Maybe I felt too young. Or it simply could have been that I was still overwhelmed by all the changes I'd experienced in such a short time." She doesn't remember specifically what made her hesitate to say yes to him—he was, after all, handsome, smart, and interesting—and yet she held back.

"I was not the type of girl who'd spent her childhood believing that once I got married, my life would be complete. Many women thought that way back then.

It wasn't that I didn't want to be married; I hoped that I would someday have a family. It's just that I was in no rush."

My grandfather, on the other hand, was very ready. Having left his homeland and his family as a teenager, he was desperate for a family in America, and tired of living alone. Shortly after Ojichan had arrived in San Francisco, he'd learned that his father had passed away. He'd decided even before the war broke out that he would never return to Japan. More than anything, he wanted to be a husband and a father, and he went to great measures to let my grandmother know he was serious.

"He could be very convincing," Obaachan says, turning to look out the window.

I remember this about my grandfather. When we were children, he would persuade us to join him in silly games with magic tricks—pretending he could pull off the upper half of his thumb was a favorite of his—and ugly masks he picked up at costume stores, chasing us around the house, roaring like a monster. At the same time, he had enough of an edge that we knew we shouldn't push our luck by mouthing off or being disrespectful. My mother had warned us not to cross the line with him.

Even as a young man, my grandfather had been persistent, and he had a way of commanding Obaachan's attention and, sometimes, of captaining her very will. He could so convincingly present an argument, even about something meaningless like the best way to cook fish, that she often found herself struggling to come up with a response. "He was much better with words than I ever was," Obaachan says as we pull into the driveway.

Depending on the day, my grandfather would alter his approach to getting her to marry him. Sometimes, he would press his hand into hers and look at her, his dark eyes dancing. It was time, he would say with tenderness. They knew each other well. They got along. They would be a good match; he promised. He was ready, and she was, too. She just didn't realize it. Besides, what was the point in waiting? Other times, when he grew frustrated, he would shrug his shoulders and kick the dust. Perhaps this was all a waste of his energy, he would say. Maybe she wasn't serious about him; maybe she was only biding time until someone better came along. The accusations would mount.

But the tactic that weighed most heavily on my grandmother's imagination was one that seemed the product of sheer desperation. Ojichan's most compelling approach was to play with her fears: there's a war going on, he would say, staring intently into her eyes, sad and serious. Who knows what will happen? In many respects, he was right.

By the fall of 1942, the war was no longer just a series of reports people listened to on their radios or watched on the newsreels at the movie theatres. For many, dim-out regulations, scrap-metal drives, air-raid alerts, and radio silence had become a part of everyday life. Automobiles, typewriters, sugar, rubber, gasoline, and fuel oil were all rationed. In the Pacific, the Battle of Guadalcanal had been raging since early August. Then, in October, the Germans and British began fighting at El Alamein in North Africa. In November, the rest of the Allies invaded North Africa in Operation Torch. Clearly, the war was growing, stretching its territory, swallowing more continents, countries, and lives. No end was in sight.

Obaachan steps out of the car. She sighs and shakes her head. "I think he knew he could get me to bend on that one. Of course I knew there was a war, and I was all too aware that my future, like everybody else's, was precarious." At the time, she worried that she might never leave Heart Mountain, that her room there might be her final one, that the image of the plains and that solitary mountain in the distance, seen through the holes of the barbed-wire fence that surrounded the camp, would be the last view she'd ever know.

Along with the uncertainty of her future, my grandmother worried as well that she might not find another person who would love her and want to marry her, like my grandfather did. She might end up alone, and many years later, wish she'd taken her chances with him. It was true that at the time, she wasn't sure that she loved him, but she knew that she cared about him, that she admired him, that she found him attractive. But was that love? She wasn't sure. What she was sure about, though, was that he loved her.

"I think that's why I said yes, in the end," Obaachan says as she walks toward the house. "I knew that he loved me. That he really, really loved me."

I remember my grandmother saying it just that way before. I suspect there was more to her decision to marry Ojichan than this—that it was not only the assurance that he loved her that led her to say yes to him. Fear about the war and the uncertainty of her future must have played a bigger role than she lets on. It strikes me as strange, too, that my grandmother does not mention her love for Ojichan when we talk about her marriage, but I don't know how to bring up this detail without somehow sounding accusatory, or worse yet, disrespectful.

By the time my grandparents would marry, on December 12, 1942, a little over a year would have passed since the bombing of Pearl Harbor. During that year, my grandmother had dropped out of college, been forced from the only home she'd ever known, lived in a whitewashed stall of a fairground barn, and resettled in a Wyoming concentration camp. I think I can understand the long shadow so much uncertainty would have cast on her, and her desire to solidify at least one small element of a life that seemed to be spinning unbearably out of her control.

Chapter 8

THE TRADITIONAL JAPANESE SYSTEM FOR ARRANGING A marriage was complicated, so my grandmother's decision to say yes to my grandfather was only the first in a series of steps leading to a wedding. First, both of my grandparents had to choose a representative, someone who could attest to their good character and respectability. Obaachan selected an older couple from Los Angeles, folks who had known her all her life and who were also interned at Heart Mountain. The couple paid a formal visit to my grandfather and assured him that Obaachan was a moral person from a solid family. Had Ojichan's parents been around, they would have been part of the conversation. Likewise, my grandfather found someone at the camp who was willing to speak to Obaachan and her parents on his behalf. He asked John Tamura, who was a "block manager" and an esteemed person at Heart Mountain, to serve as his representative. John Tamura was older, closer to Obaachan's parents in age, and his broad shoulders and straight back gave the impression of someone with dignity and authority. Also, Obaachan's parents had known him back in Los Angeles, which gave him that much more credibility in their eyes. They knew he was not simply some guy whom my grandfather had paid to speak on his behalf. They trusted Tamura's judgment. After Ojichan had been formally represented by Tamura, he had to approach Obaachan's parents himself and ask for their blessing.

Obaachan explains this system to me as we stand outside her house, in the courtyard, right after her radiation appointment. She pauses to inspect the two tomato plants she bought a few weeks earlier, kneeling and running her fingers along the slender branches and over the soft, furry leaves. A few tomatoes, still green, have grown to the size of golf balls. She pulls the planter a foot farther away from the house, out of the morning shade and into the direct sunlight. She squints, whispering to herself—she does this sometimes, to organize her thoughts, I think, but maybe also because she has lived alone now for over a decade and has learned to fill the silence with her own voice. After a moment she stands up, pulls her keys from her pocket, and walks to the front door.

"So you'd really only known Ojichan for, what, four or five months before you two were married?" I say as we step inside. I slip out of my shoes and place my purse on the floor beside me. My eyes slowly adjust to the dim lighting inside. To minimize the cost of air conditioning, Obaachan keeps the blinds closed, so it's dark in the house compared to outside in the courtyard.

She removes her red-and-tan Easy Spirit shoes in the foyer, shuffles into the kitchen, and flips on the light. "I'm not sure. Maybe seven months, maybe eight," she calls to me.

I can imagine how my own parents would have responded if, at twenty-one, I had announced I was going to marry someone I'd only known for a few months. I want to ask Obaachan whether her parents thought it was too soon, or whether they felt they didn't know my grandfather well enough to grant their blessing, or if they worried that he was too flashy and self-confident, but I realize I must handle this situation with delicacy. I don't want to offend my grandmother by asking a question she would consider inappropriate. "How did your parents feel about it?" I say carefully. "I mean, did they think it was a good idea?"

Obaachan steps out of the kitchen to look at me and sets her glass on the table in the foyer. She feels the undertones of the question. "Well," she says, "as I told you before, they liked him well enough. I know in your mind, seven months is not a very long time. And looking back, I suppose the two of us hardly knew each other. But so much had happened to us. So much was happening." She shrugs her shoulders and runs her finger along the rim of her glass. "Things are different during a war, Kimi. I guess that's the best way for you to think about it. You have to remember that the whole world was at war."

During November and December of 1942, as my grandparents followed the customary stages of an engagement as closely as they could, thousands of miles away, the Guadalcanal Campaign thundered on in the Solomons. The fighting would continue until February 9, 1943, when American troops at last took control. One of the most vicious battles of the war, the Naval Battles of Guadalcanal I and II, occurred November 12 through 15, when Japan attempted to send in reinforcements. Around four thousand of the ten thousand Japanese troops made it to the island; the others never set foot on Guadalcanal. The Americans lost nine ships; Japan lost five. Later, the Allies' victory in the Solomons would be considered the turning point in the war in the Pacific.

As battle after battle unfolded in the Pacific, and in Northern Africa and Europe, the United States continued its efforts on an altogether new and different type of weapon. In late November, the government selected

Los Alamos, New Mexico, as the site for a lab that would focus on the construction of the atomic bomb. On December 2, 1942, ten days before my grandparents' wedding, two University of Chicago physicists, Enrico Fermi and Arthur Compton, achieved the first nuclear chain reaction. A little over three years after this discovery, the United States would drop its first atomic bomb on the Japanese city of Hiroshima.

My grandparents would have kept up to date on much of the war through the newsreels the authorities showed prior to movies. In these fuzzy clips, an excited male voice narrated while bomber planes flashed across the screen, the wings dipping toward the ocean, the engines bellowing. Soldiers waved triumphantly and stood over rows of kneeling Japanese or German prisoners. And smoke poured from lush green jungles as infantry marched past, sunburned and weary.

But even within the barbed-wire confines of Heart Mountain, far away from the gunfire and sinking ships, where people were cut off, in large part, from the world, the war demanded difficult answers. A few weeks before my grandparents' wedding, in November, the authorities distributed a questionnaire—to all prisoners, both male and female—called an Application for Leave Clearance. The main purpose of this application was to determine individuals' loyalty, should any of them choose to volunteer in the war effort. Obaachan frowns as she remembers this process. "They told us to be 'as truthful as possible,'" she says, "which struck me as a strange way of putting it."

At the Heart Mountain Community Center, Obaachan sat in one of the stiff wooden chairs at a long table, reading through each question of the application carefully. She gripped the yellow pencil in her fingers, squinted at the words, and tapped the eraser lightly on the table. A guard passed by, peering over her shoulder to check on her progress. She watched him out of the corner of her eye but made sure not to turn her head.

The distribution of these questionnaires in the camps created uproar, mostly because of questions 27 and 28. Question 27 asked: "Are you willing to serve in the Armed Forces of the United States, in combat duty, wherever ordered?" Although thirty-three thousand Japanese Americans did end up serving in the US military during World War II, some people, mostly *Nisei*, or those of the second generation, found Question 27 to be offensive and unfair. Farther down the table from Obaachan, one angry young man hissed: "Why should I go put my life on the line for this country?"

"Yeah, it's like they're asking you to trade prison for a death sentence," muttered another, loudly rustling his papers.

These audacious young men made Obaachan nervous. She leaned forward, pretending to be absorbed in her survey, pressing her elbows into the table and focusing on the paper in front of her. She remembered her father's advice about following all the rules and attempting to be compliant. In two weeks, she was getting married. She didn't want to be associated with any rebels in case there was trouble. And a small part of her disapproved of their rebellious behavior—both of her brothers, after all, had jumped at the opportunity to enlist.

Question 28 created more of a stir for the *Issei*, who had been born in Japan but lived in America. Obaachan's parents were both *Issei*. It asked: "Will you swear unqualified allegiance to the United States of America and faithfully defend the United States from any or all attack by foreign or domestic forces, and forswear any form of allegiance or obedience to the Japanese emperor or any other foreign government, power, or organization?" The question was a thorny one. Its very nature put the *Issei* in an impossible situation. Like Mama and Papa, most felt loyal to the United States and considered it their home. However, despite that loyalty, they were still citizens of Japan. Forbidden by law to become US citizens—they would not, in fact, legally be permitted to become American citizens until 1954—they technically could not call the United

States their own country. Thus, the question asked them to renounce their only citizenship, to Japan, while not offering anything in return. Though they realized there might be consequences for refusing to renounce their Japanese citizenship, many also feared that if they did, after the war they would become people without a country.

Obaachan's family answered "yes" to both questions 27 and 28. In their eyes, America was their home. At the time, her parents' mind-set aligned with the creed of the Japanese American Citizens League: "to do honor to America at all times and in all places." They felt it was their duty to be at Heart Mountain—that somehow by being there they could best serve and respect their beloved country. Obaachan's sister's role was to be with her husband's family in the prison camp in Arkansas; both brothers were serving in the US military. Each of them had his or her part to play, and they had to be willing to put themselves at risk in order to do so. After all, Japanese culture emphasized community welfare over individual interests. As Obaachan's family under-stood things, it was in the community's best interest to align with America.

There were others who did not view the situation with this attitude. They believed that their rights had been violated in every sense. They wanted nothing to do with the United States and probably would have returned to Japan if given the option. A group of young men bravely—or foolishly—answered on their question-naires that they would refuse to fight for the United States but would consider fighting for Japan. They eventually became known as the "No-No Boys" because they answered "No" to question 27 and "No" to question 28 on the loyalty questionnaire. The No-No Boys were sent to the internment camp at Tule Lake, an internment camp located in California, which the War Relocation Authority decided to designate as the place where all "disloyal" interns would stay. My grandmother refers to Tule Lake as "the troublemakers' camp," a title, it seems, that would align well with how the U.S. government viewed it. Other prisoners, those who expressed a desire to return to Japan, for example, were also sent to Tule Lake. In the meantime, the "loyal" Japanese Americans who had been sent to Tule Lake when they were first evacuated were dispersed to other camps across the country. In total, around nine hundred Heart Mountain interns were sent to Tule Lake, and the same number of Tule Lake interns were moved to Heart Mountain.

"So how did Ojichan propose?" I ask, shifting subjects and looking at the thin band on my grandmother's wrinkled left hand. "Did he take you somewhere special?" I pause, realizing the strangeness of my question—is there such a thing as a "special" spot in a prison? "I mean, a place that had meaning for the two of you, there at Heart Mountain? And where did he buy the ring?"

Obaachan takes a deep breath and turns to look out the kitchen window at her grapefruit trees. "He didn't really propose, I guess." She watches as an ibis pokes about the base of a tree, submerging its long red beak into the dirt, searching. "I mean, he just kept asking, like I explained before. He tried different ways until I finally said yes."

"And the ring?"

"I got my own ring," Obaachan says, her voice very matter-of-fact. She doesn't seem troubled by the lack of romance. "He never offered to buy one."

"He didn't have money, I guess."

"It wasn't so much that. It was more just the type of person he was."

I ask her what she means.

She shrugs. "Well, he wasn't someone who would say to himself, 'I would like to get married now, but I don't have the money to buy a ring. It'll take me some time to save up for one, so we'll have to wait a few months . . .' He was impatient about most things." Obaachan looks at me then, as though trying to read my expression. "Maybe you remember that about him. Patience was not his strong suit, I guess would be a good way to put it. So saving money to order a ring and making himself wait was not an option. It probably never crossed his mind."

After all, wearing a wedding band was an American tradition that gained popularity during World War II. It was not, however, a Japanese one. Obaachan's parents didn't wear them, and my grandfather, having grown up in Japan, never wanted one. Obaachan felt differently, though. She wanted that reminder, that symbol of commitment and unity. "Plus," she adds, "in America, married women wore wedding rings. What was I going to do when I had a baby? People would see me and assume I had no husband. Back then, people were not as forgiving toward women who had children out of wedlock, you know. I would have been ashamed to walk around with my stomach out to here"—she motions, holding her arms out from her abdomen—"or later, toting children on a hip, and no ring." She shakes her head, smacking her lips. "But men don't understand these things."

My grandmother realized then that if she wanted a wedding ring, she would need to order it and pay for it herself. She remembered a popular, respected jeweler back in Los Angeles, a place right on Broadway called Slavicks, and decided to contact them from Heart Mountain. She wrote a letter detailing her situation, explaining that she needed a wedding band, and requesting that they select one in her size. To pay for it, she enclosed a $50 money order.

"It was risky," Obaachan admits, leaning against the smooth white countertop in the kitchen. "They easily could have pocketed the money and not sent anything." She straightens her white cardigan and plunges her hands into the pockets. "Especially because they would have known from my name and address that I was Japanese, and a prisoner. But they were good, honest people. And after a couple of weeks, I had a package in the mail."

She insists the ring's appearance did not matter to her and says she tried not to expect anything in particular. At the same time, Obaachan admits, she was anxious about that first look at her wedding ring. When it arrived on that cold, windy day at Heart Mountain, wrapped tidily in brown paper, she rushed back to her room to open it. Nervously, she peeled off the packaging to reveal a tiny square box. The jewelers at Slavicks had chosen a plain gold ring with a thin groove along the front that had five very small diamonds set in it. At the time, these simple rings were waning in popularity. With the luxury taxes during the war, bolder, clunkier rings with large rectangular-cut semiprecious and synthetic stones were becoming more fashionable. For Obaachan, however, the ring was perfect: simple and elegant. She tried it on, admired it, then gave it to my grandfather so he could slide it on her finger on their wedding day.

Obaachan holds out her left hand and shows me the ring. "I still like it, even today," she says, looking at the thin gold band she has now worn for over sixty years. "They did a good job picking it."

I can't help wondering how my grandfather felt about this series of events. Did he feel just a tiny bit selfish for refusing to buy my grandmother a wedding band? And knowing that she was the one who'd paid for it, did he give that ring to my grandmother with just a twinge of embarrassment on their wedding day? Did he feel cheap? And from Obaachan's perspective, I wonder whether my grandfather's lack of participation in selecting and purchasing the ring made it less meaningful. If my grandfather himself had saved his monthly earnings—and by my estimates, at Obaachan's salary of twelve dollars a month, fifty bucks was a significant sacrifice—if he had chosen the jeweler, and put forth the effort to write a letter explaining the situation, might that ring hold more significance? In addition to serving as a symbol of commitment, wouldn't it also be a sign of something my grandfather had forfeited on my grandmother's behalf? I can't ask. By the tranquil look on Obaachan's face, I can see that my grandfather's insensitivity about the wedding band is something she has long forgotten, or at least accepted.

She pulls her hand back and slides it into her pocket again. "So after I received my ring, I had other things to do to get ready. For the ceremony, I ordered a beige herringbone suit from the Montgomery Ward catalog. We had no shops besides the dry-goods store, but we had access to catalogs and could order things. The outfit wasn't very dressy, just a regular tailored suit that I could wear for other occasions afterward." She frowns and wrinkles her nose. "Buying or sewing a fancy wedding dress seemed so frivolous considering our situation. What would I do with some extravagant white dress after my wedding day? Hang it in our dusty apartment? You know I'm too practical for that, Kimi."

The man who had been Obaachan's minister at her church in Los Angeles was at Heart Mountain, and even though my grandfather was indifferent about the details of the wedding—he was not the religious type— Obaachan insisted on a formal Christian ceremony, with her minister officiating. "Before the ceremony, though, we needed to obtain a marriage license. To get this, we had to travel in a military vehicle to Cody, Wyoming, maybe twenty minutes away. A military policeman and a camp administrator had to drive us. No prisoner could ever leave Heart Mountain without a chaperone."

Their trip to Cody was the first time Obaachan had stepped foot outside of the barbed-wire confines since her arrival, four months earlier. It was also the first time she'd ridden in an automobile in what seemed like ages.

As she and my grandfather climbed into the military vehicle, she felt a tiny surge of excitement. There was something exhilarating about driving out of the camp, even though she knew it was only for a short while, and even though it was with armed chaperones. Outside of their square-mile city, she knew nothing of Wyoming. Beyond the barbed wire, what was this rugged state like? Were there mountains? Forests? Streams? She wondered if just a few miles away, the scenery might be different, with rugged, snowy mountains speckled with evergreens, like she'd seen in her schoolbooks. But her anticipation only led to disappointment. What she saw was just as dreary from outside the barbed wire as it was from within: a wide stretch of gray sky, an endless expanse of snow, and not a tree, building, or farm in sight. As they drove through the white fields, Obaachan looked back at her prison. Hundreds of long, dark buildings. A few people trudging through the snow, their navy blue peacoats wrapped tightly around them. The mountain, just beyond the camp, dark, brooding, looming like a god.

While the camp administrator, a friendly *hakujin* woman, tried to make conversation, the military policeman did not say a word during the entire trip. He sat stoically in the front seat, never taking his eyes off the road, never looking at the four Japanese prisoners in the back. Another couple was traveling to Cody as well, only they planned to pick up their license and get married that same day at the courthouse. Even though these people were complete strangers to my grandparents, they asked Obaachan and Ojichan to serve as witnesses. In the courtroom in Cody, the two of them stood a few feet behind their new acquaintances and listened as the couple exchanged vows.

On their way home, the administrator asked the military policeman to pull into the parking lot at a small liquor store. Perhaps someone had asked her if a stop would be permissible. Or maybe it was standard procedure to allow the newlyweds an opportunity to purchase a celebratory bottle of cheap champagne. My grandfather bought a bottle of whiskey for John Tamura, as a thank-you gift for helping to arrange the marriage. The other couple did not buy anything. The man at the counter, a tall, burly guy with a thick tangle of a beard, watched the four Japanese suspiciously. Obaachan avoided eye contact and stood far away from the register, her hands hidden in the deep pockets of her coat.

December 12, 1942, arrived, a bitter-cold day with sharp gales shaking the window of their small room in Block 17. Obaachan lay on her cot, tucked beneath a mound of Army-issued gray blankets. She watched as her father shoveled a heap of coal into the pot-bellied stove. Outside, fresh snow whitened the rooftops and the paths, covering the ugliness of the tar paper and rough wood, and the gloomy brown fields. On this morning, despite the low, dreary sky and the mounting snow, Obaachan was hopeful. A new chapter, one promising excitement and possibilities, lay ahead, and she felt as though she were about to embark on a great adventure. She allowed herself to believe that maybe—perhaps within a year, or even less—she and her new husband would be elsewhere, far away from Heart Mountain.

Obaachan styled her hair, powdered her face, and applied some lipstick. She put on her new beige suit and slipped her feet into a pair of brown heels. She used her small handheld mirror to check herself, moving it at various angles to piece together her overall appearance. As Obaachan knew, my grandfather valued neatly combed hair, tidy clothing, and an effort to look nice. She didn't want to disappoint him on his wedding day. Mama watched from her cot, her head resting against the white pillow, a pile of blankets heaped over her small frame.

That afternoon, the ceremony was simple: no organ or piano, no white aisle runner, no fancy veil. It was held in the big community room, the size of which made their small band of forty people seem even smaller. Chairs were set up toward the front of the room, where the minister and my grandparents stood. In the first row, Obaachan's mother, dressed in the gray tweed outfit she had worn on the day they left Los Angeles, seemed weary. Her shoulders sagged, and her clothing was now too big on her small body. Next to her, Papa looked fine in his black suit, with his hair parted and combed carefully to the side. A few silver flecks were beginning to show. Uncle Kisho, Aunt Maki, and the cousins sat behind them. Some friends came as well, young women who worked at the mess hall with Obaachan, and a handful of my grandfather's friends who'd lived with him in the bachelors' quarters. Everyone listened as the minister read from 1 Corinthians and then led my grandparents in their vows. At the back of the room, Obaachan had arranged a table with some refreshments. She had purchased some cookies from the Heart Mountain dry-goods store, as well as some fancy napkins. "It was nothing like the weddings you see today," Obaachan tells me. "Just drinks and a little bite to eat, that's it." Later that evening, all of the guests would have headed to their assigned mess halls for dinner.

After the newlyweds had greeted everyone and thanked them for coming, they left for their honeymoon—in the tiny room that used to belong to Obaachan and her parents. A few days earlier, Papa and Mama had given up that room and moved into a vacant one right across the street, in the same block. My grandparents slid the two cots together to make one big bed, but the metal edges of each were so uncomfortable that it prevented them from really being close together. As they settled into their "wedding bed," Ojichan turned out the light.

Had my grandmother known on that cold December evening just how difficult the first few years of her marriage would be, trapped in that tiny room, in a Wyoming concentration camp, she might not have felt as hopeful about what lay ahead. The war would continue for nearly three more years, and as the months stretched on, an end to the fighting and to their imprisonment felt less and less likely. In such tense conditions, despair was inevitable, listlessness was unavoidable, and tempers were bound to flare. Before long, Obaachan would see a side of my grandfather that he had managed to keep hidden throughout their brief courtship.

Chapter 9

ON THE FOURTH MORNING OF MY VISIT TO FLORIDA, Obaachan wakes up thinking of *Adam Bede*. "Only I couldn't remember part of the story," she says, shaking her head from side to side, mildly frustrated. "That's what happens when you get old. Some days, I just can't remember certain things." She smiles, shrugs her shoulders. "So I decided it was time to read it again. I do that, you know. If I forget part of a book, I'll just take it off the shelf and read it another time through." Sometimes, even if she does remember a book, she'll read it again, a second or third time, if she really likes it. *Pride and Prejudice* and *Jane Eyre* have earned multiple readings. "I've always been a reader. When we were young, my mother would take us to the public library in LA. We didn't own any books. We didn't have the money for that," she says. "And then at camp, having the library so

close was one of the few good things about being there."
She pauses for a moment, mulling over this statement,
looking down, pulling at a snag in her sweater. "Well,
that's not quite right. It was"—she nods, more certain
of this revision—"the one thing that kept me going, in
the end. Reading was what got me through."

The statement strikes me as strange. What about my
grandfather? Wouldn't the comfort of having someone
close by who loved her and understood her be what got
her through? I imagine my young grandparents, both
twenty-two years old at the time: their hair is black, not
gray, as it has always been in my memories of them, and
their faces are bright, unwrinkled, and hopeful. I see
them huddled in the stark room with its rough-cut pine
walls and its sputtering pot-bellied stove. There's something romantic about this imagined version because the
room's warm and it's more a cabin than a prison, and
they're leaning into each other, seated on the low cots,
my grandmother's head resting on Ojichan's shoulder.

But this is how I want to see them, not how they
were. This is a version I've concocted in my imagination
after too many Hollywood films and Victorian novels. I
wish I could press Obaachan for an explanation—some
details of this life in the winter months of 1943, some
hint of why she calls reading the one thing that got her
through—but I don't. I sense that she is in some way
protecting my grandfather, that she doesn't want me

to think poorly of him, that perhaps her unwillingness to go into details about his shortcomings is a way of showing her love for him. I understand now, too, that this game of ours, of going through and reconstructing the particulars, is one of give and take. If I try to take too much, if I push in the wrong places, she'll shut down; she won't give. And I'll never learn the rest of what happened to her.

Obaachan had known for some time that the Heart Mountain library was scheduled to open because she'd read an announcement on the community bulletin board, and on the day of its opening, she was there, standing in the cold, her feet shifting anxiously on the packed snow. To her surprise, the library was not stocked with only used books that had been discarded or donated; many of them were new. Tall, simple shelves stretched the length of the small room, and books of all genres filled the spaces.

Obaachan would almost always go for the fiction; her favorites were novels with love stories and strong women characters who stood up for what they believed in and who, by the book's end, married someone they adored. I find my grandmother's literary preferences a little surprising, since she herself claims to have been too practical for romance and too weak to stand up to anyone. But I choose not to point this out. She's aware,

I think, of the discrepancy between her own life and the lives of her heroines.

At Heart Mountain, Obaachan continued her work at the mess hall, in the same position she had at the Pomona Fairground, which included distributing each prisoner's rationed amount of sugar, as well as helping with cleanup duties. Her days revolved around three two-hour shifts, but in between meals, she had to find ways to keep busy. Chores—sweeping the dust that slipped beneath the door and into the room, washing their clothes, and ironing—took up a handful of hours each week, but she still had a good deal of free time.

Had it not been for the library, my grandmother might have picked up a hobby like crocheting or the Japanese art of flower arrangement, *ikebana*, as many of her fellow prisoners did, but books proved to be too tempting a diversion from the tedium of life. Although she had taken an embroidery class at Pomona, she did not enroll in any courses at Heart Mountain. Whereas many women at Heart Mountain loved the opportunity to attend a class and catch up on the latest camp gossip, my grandmother preferred reading to such communal activities precisely because it did not require socializing. Even today she admits that she prefers the solitude of a book to social gatherings. More importantly, though, she loved the experience of opening a brand-new book, the feel of the spine cracking just a little, the smell of crisp paper. She loved placing my grandfather's pillow on top of her own, and settling onto her cot for an afternoon of reading. As the wind raged outside her room, she burrowed herself under her heavy wool blankets, escaping, if only in twenty-minute stints, her life in Wyoming.

"The book I remember having the biggest impact on me was *The Fountainhead* by Ayn Rand," Obaachan says. "Have you read it?"

"No," I tell her.

"You haven't?" she says, both surprised and disappointed. She seems to assume, like many people, that because I majored in English, I've read everything. "Well, you should, Kimi. You would like it. You see, the hero—he refused to be persuaded by the pressures of those around him. He was so unlike me," Obaachan says, folding her hands. "He was so strong, so committed to being himself, no matter the cost." She shakes her head. "I was just the opposite. I went with the flow. I did everything I could to follow other people's rules and demands." She frowns and looks at me, and although she doesn't say it, I sense that she wants to tell me to be the architect in that novel, to be true to myself. To make sure I am not like her.

Obaachan, I perceive in this moment, is failing to figure into this harsh self-judgment just how bleak her situation was, not only as a Japanese American growing up in a blatantly racist California, but as a woman. Even before Pearl Harbor, her choices were limited in terms of career and lifestyle, and when the war broke out, those options became even more limited. She was told where and how to live; when, where, and what to eat; where to shower; what to do. And just as Obaachan was beginning to settle into the rules and expectations at Heart Mountain—about five months into her stay—she had to adjust to the demands of her new husband.

He turned out to be a difficult roommate and an exacting partner. Compared to Obaachan's father, whose quiet, calm ways had set the tone for their life on Pico Street and even in Pomona and Wyoming, Ojichan was a taxing, powerful force, who insisted that things go his way all the time. Although Papa had been the designated leader of the household, he would ask his wife for her opinion and would always act in her best interest. My grandfather, on the other hand, knew nothing of compromise and would raise his voice to drown out Obaachan's if he felt he had a point to make. He refused to admit mistakes and ran circles around her with his affection for debate. He meddled in my grandmother's chores and fussed about each and every task she took on. On more than one occasion, he followed her to the laundry room.

"When you press my shirts," Ojichan would say, gripping the iron and tipping it toward his favorite light blue dress shirt, "only starch the front and the collar. The back doesn't need starch. It's a waste to spray it there."

My grandmother wouldn't argue.

"And when you iron the collar, you need to do it like this," he would continue, again demonstrating. "Start on each end and meet in the middle. If there's going to be a crease in the fabric, it should be in the back, where people are less likely to notice. I hate it when people have creases in their collars. It looks so sloppy."

"Okay," Obaachan would say, stealing a self-conscious glance around the room.

This was another one of my grandfather's lessons. Although he often ironed his own shirts, he wanted to make sure Obaachan knew how to do it to his specifications—hence, the tutorial in the laundry room. Obaachan found the "lesson" demeaning and irritating: there were other women around, and who knew what they were thinking as they watched a husband teach his wife how to iron a shirt. No other husbands frequented the laundry room to give their wives ironing instructions. It was embarrassing. Obaachan felt as though every woman in that room must have deemed her incompetent. Of course, she'd learned to iron from her mother—Obaachan had, after all, been taking care of her family's household duties for nearly a decade before she'd gotten married—but apparently her skills were not up to Ojichan's standards.

"My Papa never made a big deal out of dress or appearance. He always looked nice, but he was not the type to fuss about creases or fashion or starch," Obaachan explains, shaking her head. It did not take long for her to realize that the very thing she'd found attractive in my grandfather as a suitor—his style and handsome appearance—was maddening in a husband.

In Florida, Obaachan and I are returning from another radiation appointment. She must go five days a week for two months; she is now on her third week. On our way home, we swing by the supermarket, Publix. Today, she's making subs for lunch, and we're taking them to the beach because it's the last day of my visit, and I've been wanting to go all week. As we walk through the store, Obaachan's red purse is tucked carefully beneath her left arm. I was the one who taught her, she recently told me when I commented on it, that a handbag does not need to match an outfit perfectly. For a woman who rarely wears shades other than gray, blue, and white, the red purse is an unexpected splash of color.

"They make the best subs in South Jersey," she remembers as we walk through the produce department of

Publix. "Nothing compares." After my grandparents were released from Heart Mountain, that's where they moved, to the East Coast, to work at Seabrook Farms, a company that had recruited Japanese prisoners from the camps to join its workforce. They didn't leave New Jersey until they were in their seventies, when they moved to Florida.

She inspects a vine-ripened tomato, gently pressing her fingertips against the skin. "Too bad my tomatoes aren't ready yet." She places the tomato in a clear plastic bag and drops it into the shopping cart. We gather up the rest of our ingredients, the thin-sliced baked ham, the salami, provolone, and sub rolls, and head home. In her kitchen Obaachan carefully assembles the sandwiches, using a brush to cover the rolls with olive oil and oregano. She packs them in her old blue-and-white cooler and adds two ice packs and two cans of Coke. "We don't need potato chips, right?" she calls to me. I am searching her linen closet, near the front door, for two beach towels. "They're unhealthy," she adds. "And I don't have any here." She chuckles at the order of her own sentences. "I guess I shouldn't have asked, huh? Since I have nothing to offer."

"I don't need chips," I call to her loudly, turning to face the kitchen, so that she can hear with her one good ear. I roll up the towels I've grabbed from the linen closet and shove them into my small beach bag. I carry the first load of items to the car.

"We need the beach umbrella," Obaachan yells from the house. "It's in the corner, by Ojichan's old work table. I can't be in the sun," she says. "I don't take a sunbath like you." I smile at the strange diction. Even though my grandmother has been speaking strictly English for decades, every once in a while she pieces sentences together in odd ways. I grab the umbrella and the two canvas beach chairs, place them in the trunk, then walk back to the house and tell her I'm ready. Obaachan stands in the doorway, her wide-brimmed white sunhat pulled low over her forehead. In the sunshine, her Transitions lenses grow darker.

At Satellite Beach we carry our things down the worn wooden steps to the sand and then set up the umbrella so that Obaachan can sit in complete shade. As with her diet and exercise, my grandmother is fastidious about sun exposure. She uses sunblock every day and wears a hat anytime she's in the sun. It still seems strange to me that a person so conscientious about her health can be battling cancer. What makes my grandmother's cancer even stranger is that she seems outwardly unaffected by it. In moments, I forget. In other moments, I am keenly aware that just a few months earlier, they found a lump in her breast during her annual exam, and that they dug the cells and flesh from her left side—that a small part of her has been removed.

Obaachan sorts through the cooler and hands me a sandwich. She takes out her own lunch, opens a napkin, and spreads it across her lap. "Shortly after we got married," she says as she cracks open a Coke, "your grandfather came up with this idea that we had to have a wedding picture."

Months after the actual ceremony, in the spring of 1943, my grandfather, following some sentimental impulse, announced that it was unacceptable that he and Obaachan lacked a formal wedding picture. He arranged to borrow an acquaintance's camera, and informed my grandmother that she had to come up with a wedding gown for the photograph.

"We need something to show our children," my grandfather insisted. "We can't just tell them we got married in camp. They'll want to see a picture of us. And we just won't tell them that it was taken much later. They'll assume it was taken on our wedding day, and we'll let them assume that . . ."

My grandmother was resistant, disliking how contrived the whole thing was, but she was too nervous to go against her new husband's wishes. She wrote her sister a letter asking to borrow her wedding dress—Sachiko had taken it to Arkansas with her—and when the gown arrived in the mail, Obaachan rolled her straight hair into pin curls, brushed on some rouge, slid on some red lipstick, and put on her sister's gown. They were the same height and wore the same size, so the dress fit quite well.

"At the time, your grandfather was developing an interest in photography. If he could have done anything in the world he wanted, he would have been a professional photographer," Obaachan says. She looks down, folds her hands at her waist. "But after the war—well— we all made sacrifices." In their room at Heart Mountain, Ojichan set up a white sheet for the backdrop. He thought it through: the lighting, the pose, the angle. He was very meticulous about it. Obaachan smiles. "He wanted the memento to be perfect."

Or *seem* perfect, I think to myself. Although I say nothing of this to Obaachan, I find my grandfather's endeavor to capture his marriage like this both moving and troubling. I appreciate that he thought of his children, and grandchildren, and that he considered how one day that photograph would become a family relic. And yet, another part of me can't help thinking of my grandfather's careful reconstruction of his wedding day as some misguided attempt to make their history more palatable to us, more pleasant. Less a source of *haji* for everyone—but also less honest.

"He was a perfectionist," Obaachan says, adjusting her chair so that it sinks deeper into the sand. "He wanted things to be done his way. He was also obsessed with hygiene. And he expected the same of me." Once, on a hot summer day, he was walking beside her, and when he reached out and felt that her arm had grown sticky in the heat, he shuddered in disgust. You need to take a shower, he told her. You're *neba-neba*. Sticky.

Obaachan shakes her head and smacks her lips. "His thinking was that if you sweat, your skin was no longer clean. And if it wasn't clean, you needed to shower." It was not unusual for my grandfather to shower and change clothes a couple times a day. His obsession with cleanliness must have become annoying pretty quickly, especially because laundry at Heart Mountain involved hauling the clothes, sheets, or towels to and from the public laundry room, a city block away. Plus, the ever-present dust made cleaning the room an almost futile endeavor.

"And he used to polish his shoes every afternoon." Obaachan stretches out her legs and looks at her sneakers. Even at the beach, she does not wear sandals. They are not supportive enough for her feet, and she is too practical to choose style over comfort. "He was so obsessive about things," she adds. "And there, with all that dust and snow, nobody cared. No one looked at your shoes. I wanted to ask him, 'Who are you trying to impress anyway?' We were prisoners, after all. But he would've been very upset if I had said that. He didn't like smart remarks." She rests her feet in the sand and looks out at the water. "I learned that the hard way," she says.

They were talking about shoes. She had just returned from doing laundry, and as she stepped into the apartment, her arms loaded with Ojichan's white shirts and a few of her own cotton blouses, my grandfather was polishing his shoes. He had his little stool on the ground and his box of polishes on the table, and he glanced up when she came to the door, not all the way up, but at her shoes.

"You need to polish those," he said. It was a command, not an observation. "People will judge you by your shoes. I've told you that a hundred times before." He continued rubbing the tip of his brown leather loafers, examining them closely, turning the shoe to check each angle for scuffs. His cigarette lay in the ashtray, a furl of smoke rising from its end.

"Oh, what do you care?" Obaachan said to him, under her breath, not looking at him. She marched the laundry over to the cots and dumped the shirts. She was tired and out of breath from the long walk, and she was not in the mood for lessons or antics. But as soon as she'd said it, she knew she'd made a mistake.

My grandfather flew into a fury. He stood up from the table, grabbed his box of polishes, and flung it across the room. Around he went, picking up any loose item he could get his hands on, heaving it against a wall. A newspaper fluttered apart. Obaachan's mug crashed to the floor and shattered into hundreds of white shards. A library book thumped hideously against the wooden wall. She was speechless. If she had not been completely paralyzed with fear and shock, she would have offered an apology, but no words would form in her mouth. After a few moments, Ojichan headed for the door and walked out, slamming it with such force that the flimsy walls shook and Obaachan was sure the neighbors had paused to wonder what was going on. In the silence he left behind him, she at last found her breath and sighed. When she looked down, she saw that her hands were shaking against her dress. She never defied my grandfather again, she tells me—not for the rest of her life.

As my grandmother shares these pieces of her early months of marriage at Heart Mountain, I think about how the Obaachan I knew as a child stood in my grandfather's shadow, head lowered, eyes turned down. How she never interrupted or corrected him, and how she moved about the house tending to her chores, in silence. Of course, her desire to appease my grandfather was no reason for her to keep her distance from us, but perhaps she simply learned not to encroach on his territory—in this case, playing with and teaching the grandchildren— in order to maintain harmony. As I learn more about their life together, I think I begin to understand why she didn't mention her marriage as the thing that sustained her through the hardships of prison life. In those winter months of 1943, Obaachan must have hoped that getting married would somehow ease the pain of how much she had lost—the chance to attend college, the siblings who'd been scattered across the country. After all, most people get married with the anticipation that life will be relatively happy. Instead, my grandfather merely brought more demands and regulations. In a way, by getting married, my grandmother had only created another prison for herself.

The sun has shifted on Satellite Beach, and Obaachan reaches out and moves the position of the umbrella so that every inch of her body remains in the shade. A white-haired man has found a fishing spot nearby, closer to the water, and he sorts through his brown tackle box, pulls out a sinker, and opens a clear plastic container of squid. Watching him, Obaachan smiles.

"Your grandfather loved surf fishing," she says. "Do you remember? Sometimes he would take your brother with him when the two of you visited. He knew your brother was like him, most alive at the shore, facing the water. He looked forward to taking him." She smiles at the memory.

I remember those childhood trips to the beach: the tall rod plugged into the PVC pipe, shoved into the ground, and my grandfather, lanky and straight, standing beside it, his hand shading his eyes, squinting at the gleaming water. And my brother dashing up and down the shore, kicking the water, throwing shells at the gulls that swept close enough to be a temptation. Ojichan would watch the rod's end as it dipped and danced with the waves. He knew enough about angling and the ocean to sense when it was a fish latching onto the bait, and when it was just the undertow tugging at the line.

"It wasn't all bad," Obaachan says resolutely. "I don't want you to think that." She frowns, looking at the fisherman. He baits his line, double-checks the heavy sinkers, and casts way out at the breakers. "It was an adjustment, being married to your grandfather. That's all." The whole experience—being in the camp, being far from all that was familiar—was an adjustment. She missed the warmth of Los Angeles, the sweet smell of camellias and forsythia from Papa's garden, the fresh bamboo shoots, and Sunday afternoons at Brighton Beach, with Mama's set of stackable containers and hot dogs roasting after the sun set. While Obaachan insists that life wasn't all bad, and while she seems to have a few good memories, I'm not convinced that she's being entirely honest in this moment. It feels like she might be trying to protect my grandfather. And maybe protecting me, too, from realizing that the man I have such fond memories of, the man who, in many ways, was an ideal grandfather, had a side to him that was not so positive.

In Wyoming, the winter could drag on for nine months, with the snow falling and drifting and piling up along the barracks. Obaachan grew tired of having to walk cautiously along the icy paths, and of having to clean up the chunks of snow that fell from their boots each time they came into the apartment. She hated worrying about that coal stove—there had been so many fires, flames swallowing the buildings and everything within.

To add to the stress of their first few months together, shortly after my grandparents' wedding, Obaachan's Mama took a turn for the worse. Living at Heart Mountain had never been easy for her or Papa. Mama's activity outside of her room was limited to occasional trips to the bathrooms to bathe. Obaachan would gather up the soap, shampoo, towels, and clean clothing for her mother, then walk the hundred yards to the bathrooms to draw her a bath. Although most prisoners showered instead of taking a bath, there were tubs in one section for those who were unable to take a regular shower.

Even Mama's meals were taken in the room. She would not have been able to walk all the way to the mess hall. The harsh temperatures alone would have been taxing for her, not to mention the high winds and icy walkways.

Obaachan's Mama did not eat the same meals that the rest of the prisoners ate. Because of her heart condition, she was served healthier food from a specially cooked menu that the camp's nutritionist had designed for people with poor health. Obaachan remembers toasting the slice of bread that Mama often saved for her, as a snack, later in the evening. She used the hot plate Papa had purchased right before they left Los Angeles and smeared a teaspoon of jelly, also from Mama, on top.

Papa was the one who took care of getting Mama her meals. Three times a day, Papa took a plate, bowl, and cup to the mess hall to pick up her food. After the workers dished out her special meal, he carefully wrapped it in a giant blue handkerchief to try to keep it warm, and then rushed it back to the apartment. Once Mama had been taken care of, Papa went back to the mess hall to eat his own food, alone. Usually, he could not stay with her while she ate because in the meantime, the mess hall would stop serving, and he would miss his meal. Obaachan worked during all the meals, so she was never available to help with Mama's food.

"Meals were difficult," Obaachan says, running her finger along the metal edge of her beach chair. "In Los Angeles, I never appreciated sitting at the kitchen table with my family for dinner. I never gave it a thought. But then, at Heart Mountain, when we had to stand in those long lines, and eat whatever they gave us, and eat at a certain time, not when you were hungry, but when the cafeteria was open . . ." She shakes her head, twisting her mouth in distaste. "After awhile, I just hated it."

I think of my first few weeks at Messiah College, and how on certain days the smell of the Lottie Nelson Dining Hall would nauseate me when I walked through the doors. Chicken-fried steak was the source of the stench, I think. (We didn't know if it was chicken or steak.) And some attempt at Mediterranean-style fish, with tomatoes and chickpeas. Those two were the worst. I often ate salad and softserve— but at least I had choices, different stations, sandwiches, soups, pizza. I remember missing my parents' meals, and the intimacy of the island in their kitchen, where we had most of our dinners. After a semester, I was convinced I could cook better meals in the dormitory kitchen and began begging my mother to get me off the meal plan. As I imagine my grandmother at Heart Mountain, I wonder if part of the reason why she is so meticulous about what she eats now is because she spent three years eating whatever was scooped onto her tray.

"It was hard on my father," Obaachan says, her voice stiff and quiet. "Taking the meals three times a day, emptying the chamber pot each morning. He never complained, never showed anger or frustration."

She turns to look at me and smiles a little. "He was not like your Ojichan."

Even when the minister, the man renting their house back in Los Angeles, began to swindle them, Papa showed no anger. Obaachan's family never saw the minister again after they parted ways on that April morning, on the sidewalk of Pico Street. The arrangement he and Papa had agreed to was that after they reached their final destination, Obaachan would write to the minister and give him their permanent address. The minister promised to mail the rent check at the beginning of each month. This agreement, however, did not end up as Papa had envisioned.

When Obaachan received the first of the minister's letters, she discovered that only a portion of the amount he and Papa had agreed upon was enclosed. She read the note and translated it, explaining to her father what the minister had written and why he had not paid the full amount: the heater, according to the minister, had stopped working, and he had been forced to hire someone to fix it. The minister had deducted the amount he supposedly paid for this service from the rent money. Papa only nodded as Obaachan read the letter, but he seemed perplexed that the heater had broken since it had hardly ever been used. Heaters, as Obaachan understood but did not state aloud, were rarely needed in Southern California.

When the second letter arrived, Obaachan again translated it to her father. This time, the minister explained that the refrigerator had stopped working, and once again the full amount owed was not paid. Again, Papa said nothing. When Obaachan opened the third letter to discover that there had been some plumbing issues, and that the rent payment had yet again been reduced, she grew angry. She knew the man was being dishonest about the problems at the house—Papa had always been fastidious about keeping it in perfect working order—and yet she was hesitant to accuse a minister of deceit. Surely a preacher would not lie to them. Surely the leader of a church would feel guilty about cheating them of what little they were asking from him. She wanted to believe that the man was a scrupulous person. But she knew deep down that the minister was indeed cheating her family. Despite his apologies that April morning when Papa handed him the keys, the sympathetic look in his wife's brown eyes as they left, and the fact that he was a preacher, he was obviously taking advantage of their imprisonment and the fact that they had absolutely no recourse if he chose to underpay them. In the end, over the three years Obaachan's family spent at Heart Mountain, the minister never once sent the full amount.

"Ojichan would not have stood for that kind of behavior the way my father did," Obaachan says. "He would have had a fit." She kicks at the sand, shrugs her shoulders, then looks at me with her eyebrows raised. "But then, he only would have caused himself more stress. There was nothing we could do about it. Who would we tell? Papa understood that we were helpless, that no one had time to listen to our complaints." They were prisoners, the lowest of the low. And it was wartime.

"*Shikataganai*," Obaachan says with a faint smile. There are things that cannot be changed, and you don't try to change them. You make the best of your situation and keep your head held high.

As I watch my grandmother on this warm March afternoon, and see the acquiescence in her eyes and the sense of calm with which she tells the story, I realize that *shikataganai* is not the same word for me as it was a few years earlier, when she first taught it to me. It's no longer just the state of mind that prevented my grandmother and her family from resisting their imprisonment sixty years ago. It's no longer a simple act of throwing in the towel or giving up—not exactly. It's that the family resigned themselves to their fate, and in that way, strangely, managed to preserve their dignity, their humanity, and, most importantly, their sense of self. This same mind-set of *shikataganai* is the one that allows my grandmother to move on with her life after a lumpectomy and a series of physical therapy visits, to sit on a beach with me just hours after a draining radiation treatment, to drive herself to the next appointment, and the one after that, morning after morning, even when I have flown home to Pennsylvania, and left her.

Chapter 10

OBAACHAN HAS KILLED A SNAKE. SHE'D JUST RETURNED from the library in Melbourne, and as she made her way across her courtyard, she saw it, thin and green, stretched across the bright concrete, warming itself in the sun. She didn't know what kind of snake it was, its breed or name, but she knew immediately that she had to kill it. She explains this as we walk through her courtyard and into the house, a year after my last visit, in March again. I follow her, rolling my small suitcase noisily over the concrete. Oddly, I find myself responding like a fretting mother to her story: Doesn't she know how many poisonous snakes there are in Florida? Couldn't she have called her neighbor, the nice Colombian man she refers to as "such a gentleman"? And what would she have done if the snake had struck her?

"It was the size of a fat man's thumb," she says, ignoring my concerns. She holds her own small thumb at arm's length, showing me. "I knew I only had one chance to kill it. If I didn't, who knows where it might show up." Once, she found one of the lizards that are so abundant in central Florida on her pillow, its brown legs extended, its skinny tail twitching. Somehow, it had squeezed its way into the house, through a crack in the foundation, or a space in the painted cedar siding. Knowing that the snake could do the same thing— surprise her somewhere inside with a flash of its shiny green skin, or worse, a bite—was enough to prompt action.

In the courtyard, Obaachan watched the snake for a few moments, then crept toward the garage and grabbed a shovel. "I had to line up my angle," she says, pointing to where the snake had lain. "I had to think through how I'd do it, and then concentrate." She inched closer to the snake, which still lay in the corner of the court-yard, right beside her tomato plants. She swung the shovel, its metal ringing loudly off the concrete, and then she continued to strike the snake, again and again. In moments it lay dead in two green pieces, splattered in blood, the thin bones exposed, the head severed.

"Afterward, I had to get the hose and clean up the blood," Obaachan says. She frowns, mildly disgusted by this part of the event, all the carnage splayed across her entryway. "I hooked the snake over my shovel and carried it out to the end of the driveway, where the trash can was. I showed my neighbor. He was working in his yard and so I called out to him, 'Hey, look at this!' and he came over and couldn't believe I'd killed it on my own."

I've witnessed this ruthless side of my grandmother only once, when she used a spray bottle of Windex to "stun" a lizard perched on her living-room windowsill, before finishing the job with the yellow fly swatter she keeps under the kitchen sink. But still, a snake is different from a lizard, more sinister and unnerving, more of a threat, and picturing my gray-haired, hundred-pound grandmother clubbing a snake to death with a garden shovel is somehow comical, bewildering, and impressive, all at once.

"I used to be afraid of snakes," she says, placing her red purse on the glass table in the courtyard. She steps into the shade of the house and uses her foot to straighten the doormat. "At Heart Mountain, I remember that your grandfather wanted to hike out across the desert and up to the mountain, but people always talked about seeing rattlesnakes up there in all the rocks, and I was scared."

Prisoners were permitted to hike out to Heart Mountain, the tall, rocky hill after which the camp was named, and many did. It was, aside from heading to Cody to obtain a marriage license from the justice of the peace or joining a work crew to pick sugar beets in Montana, one of the few opportunities the prisoners would have had to step beyond the barbed wire. The guards, armed with their machines guns, could see the venturing prisoners from their tall watchtowers, and with so many miles of desert surrounding the camp on all sides, everyone knew the prisoners' chances of surviving an escape attempt were slim. In the four years Heart Mountain remained open, no one even tried, although a sixty-three-year-old chef was shot to death by a sentry who claimed he thought the man was trying to escape. (It was later discovered that the old man had been inside the barbed-wire fence, and facing the guard.)

"Put on your most comfortable pair of shoes," Ojichan told my grandmother one warm summer afternoon, standing in the doorway of their room, the sun at his back, his khakis clean and starched, his tall, knee-high leather boots polished and bright. "And pants," he added, glancing at the white cotton skirt that fell just below her knees. "You need pants. We're going for a hike."

Obaachan obediently placed her work aside. She knew better than to tell him she didn't feel like trekking out to the mountain in the hot, dry heat; that she was nervous about the rattlesnakes young men liked to kill, bring home, and spread out on their rickety front porches for spectators; that she saw no point in getting a bird's-eye view of their prison. His words, she understood, were more a command than an invitation. So she stood up and asked Ojichan to close the door while she changed.

"What are you working on now?" he asked, shutting the door and walking toward her to check out the thin piece of cloth she'd laid aside on her cot.

"Another belt," she said. She was referring to a Belt of a Thousand Stitches, or *senninbari*, an old Japanese tradition. Whenever a man went off to war, someone from home—a wife, mother, or sister—would cut a sash of cloth, and pass it around to various women. Each person was to sew a single stitch in the fabric, so that, in total, there were a thousand stitches by a thousand different people. The soldier would then wear the belt at all times, and the belief was that it would protect him from harm and guarantee safe return. These belts circulated frequently, my grandmother remembers, from friends and friends of friends, and over her years at Heart Mountain, Obaachan ended up sewing her single stitch into a number of them.

"I never asked which side they were fighting for," Obaachan tells me, her voice low and secretive, as though realizing maybe she did something wrong all

those years ago. She shrugs, still standing in the courtyard, her Transitions lenses growing dark in the bright
light. "Maybe I was sewing stitches in a belt that would
end up being for someone fighting for Japan. It was not
the kind of thing I could ask, really. It would've been
inappropriate. If a woman asked me to do my part, I
stitched and passed it on to the next person. I didn't ask
questions."

It's very unlikely—impossible, rather—that my
grandmother was stitching belts for someone fighting
for Japan. Instead, she was likely stitching for one of the
twenty-five thousand Japanese Americans who participated in the US war effort. All of them, whether volunteers or draftees, fought in their own segregated unit,
one comprised only of *Nisei*. The all-Japanese 442nd
Regimental Combat Team had to work hard to earn
the respect—and trust—of their fellow *hakujin* soldiers
during the war. However, after liberating the town of
Bruyères in Northeastern France and rescuing the "Lost
Battalion," they did gain that respect, at least within
the military. Overall, eighteen thousand total awards
were bestowed upon the 442nd, including ninety-five
hundred Purple Hearts, fifty-two Distinguished Service
Crosses, and seven Distinguished Unit Citations. To
this day, the 442nd remains the most decorated military unit in American history. Over nine hundred men
and women from the Heart Mountain camp served on

America's behalf in the war, so many of the belts my grandmother stitched would have been sent to a friend's nephew or son, maybe even someone she'd seen in the mess hall or movie theatre.

Besides, prisoners were not permitted to send any mail to Japan, which is why so many families lost touch with their Japanese friends and relatives during the forties. And all mail, incoming and outgoing, was read by the authorities and checked for signs of espionage or language that appeared suspicious. When my grandmother received letters from her sister, the seal was broken and taped shut. When the African American minister's mail arrived, it, too, had clearly been read. Everything my grandparents sent from Heart Mountain would have been checked as well. The authorities weren't willing to take any chances with their prisoners—no "Jap" could be trusted.

Despite the fact that the Axis was facing major losses on all three fronts through the summer of 1943—the Allies were targeting mainland Greece and Italy, and the Soviets defeated the Germans in the Battle of Kursk—and despite the fact that the tide of the war had clearly turned in favor of the Allies, the American view of the Japanese was not growing any less harsh. After all, the war against the Japanese in the Pacific had by this point become known as "A War without Mercy." An example of the American attitude toward the Japanese could be summarized by the words of the controversial but ever-popular Admiral William "Bull" Halsey, who explained that his formula in the war was to "Kill Japs, kill Japs, and keep on killing Japs."

In her room at Heart Mountain, Obaachan slipped from her skirt, folded it, and placed it neatly on her cot while my grandfather waited by the door. She eased her feet into a pair of thick wool socks, grabbed a pair of pants from her shelf, and selected a pair of shoes to wear for the hike. She wore a wide-brimmed hat, too, to protect her skin from the intense Wyoming sun.

There are photographs of this day in the sparse album of my grandparents' early years as a married couple. Obaachan, lipsticked and pretty, her hair shoulder length and wavy from the pin curls she slept in each night, sitting on a boulder, her legs stretched out, crossed at the ankles, her head tilted back, her chin high, like the pictures of movie stars from that era. Ojichan, standing, one foot resting on a rock, the tall leather boots dark against his light clothing, his collared shirt unbuttoned at the top, his face young and serious, but happy. High up on the mountain, there is no barbed wire in sight.

However, excursions like the one in the photograph were rare for my grandparents. As each month of 1943 passed, they continued to settle into the monotony of life at Heart Mountain, which over time began to function much like a small city. (With a population of 10,800, it was, in fact, the third largest "city" in Wyoming from 1942 to 1945.) Work helped distract them and provided structure. My grandfather tended to grow tired of the tedious jobs available at Heart Mountain rather quickly, and switched positions often. He worked as a block manager for awhile, served as a clerk in the electricity department, and eventually traveled on the work crews that occasionally left Heart Mountain. Obaachan continued to work the same job she'd had at Pomona, in the mess hall, through the entirety of the war.

Neither of them would have made much money in their jobs. The War Relocation Authority made a rule that no Japanese could earn more than a private in the army, whose salary was $21 a month. This rule applied to everyone, including teachers, nurses, and even medical doctors. Most of the prisoners were paid between $12 and $19 per month. Obaachan and Ojichan, both of whom would have been considered unskilled laborers, would have been in the $12 category. Generally, prisoners at Heart Mountain were expected to work forty-eight hours a week. In Obaachan's case, that meant three short shifts a day, at breakfast, lunch, and dinner, seven days a week. Many prisoners, like my grandmother's family, who never would have complained about inequity, accepted their meager wages without protest. However, the discrepancy was obvious.

For instance, while internee doctors were paid $19 a month at Heart Mountain, Caucasian nurses working at the same hospital earned $150 per month. At the Heart Mountain schools, Japanese American teachers faced similar discrimination, earning $228 a year, while Caucasian instructors were paid between $2,000 and $2,600 annually.

My grandmother had never had a real job before becoming a prisoner, since she took care of her mother full-time after finishing high school, so she tells me she remembers being somewhat excited about having a source of income, rather than annoyed by the low wages. Her housing, food, and medical needs were paid for, so with her $12 a month, she was able to purchase things like clothing, snack food, toiletries, and other items. Plus, she had been raised without many luxuries, so limited money was not much of an issue for her.

Each morning, Obaachan got up and headed to the Block 17 mess hall to measure out and then distribute to each prisoner the rationed one teaspoon of sugar. Her supervisor there was a young woman named Yoshi, and she was a few years older than the rest of the workers, probably around age twenty-four or twenty-five. Although Yoshi was not pretty, she was thin, had noticeably good posture, and moved with grace and confidence. While most of the workers had very little experience in food service, Yoshi had worked as a waitress back in California, prior to coming to Heart Mountain. She was very professional, and she was the type of person who would have embraced any job earnestly, whether it was in a prison mess hall or a fancy restaurant.

"If jelly is served, you must wipe the rim of the jar before putting the lid back on," Yoshi explained during orientation, efficiently wiping all the spilled jam from a jar, then replacing the lid. "Make sure the lid is on tight, too. We don't want to create more of a mess for ourselves, and we certainly don't have food to waste.

"Waitresses," she said, looking at her staff of young women, "as you know, during the meal you'll be serving drinks. Politely ask people what they would like. Pay special attention to the elderly. Make sure you always ask them if they are in need of anything. It is our duty to be helpful and courteous to every single person who steps into this room, even those who are not always courteous to us in return. Does everyone understand this?" At that point, Obaachan and the rest of the crew nodded, half nervous, half mesmerized by the young woman's poise and her comfort in commanding an audience. As a Japanese woman in the 1940s, Yoshi would have been unusual. Even the young men who served as busboys did not dare cross her or question her orders.

"I would not say that we all liked her—or disliked her, for that matter—but we did respect her," Obaachan explains. "If a waitress had a difficult person at one of her tables, Yoshi would step in to help mediate. If someone was getting behind, she would help the person catch up. So I guess she was a good boss."

The mess halls at Heart Mountain received their food supply from a number of sources. Milk came from a creamery in nearby Powell, and the camp did rely on canned goods for many of its meals. However, the camp also produced a good bit of its own food. For political reasons, the War Relocation Authority wanted to make the camp as self-sufficient as possible. If they purchased the food locally, the locals would resent losing their own sources. If they purchased it from outside the area, the locals would be angry that the local economy was not being supported. The best option, politically, was for Heart Mountain to produce at least some of its own food.

In the spring of 1943, a few months after my grandparents' wedding, farming efforts began. First, the prisoners completed the Heart Mountain Division of the Shoshone Irrigation Project, helping with sixteen hundred feet of a five thousand-foot canal. This project, still in use today, allows barley to grow where the barracks of the prison once were. The prisoners' next task was to clear several thousand acres of sagebrush so that cabbage, peas, beans, carrots, cantaloupe, watermelon, and other fruits and vegetables could be grown. Although the locals believed that crops could not grow in that part of Wyoming and actually laughed at the idea, the prisoners embraced the challenge and were able to transform the dry ground into fertile soil. That first autumn harvest yielded 1,065 tons of produce; the next year was even better, with twenty-five hundred tons harvested. Heart Mountain also raised cattle, pigs, and chicken for its own use, all on land that had been semidesert prior to the irrigation project.

Late in the afternoon, in Florida, Obaachan calls me into her bedroom. She has recently purchased a new bedspread and wants to show me. "I'm going green," she says with a sly grin, pointing to her bed, with its light and dark green squares. I run my hand along the stitching and tell her I like it very much. She shrugs. "It was time for a change." My uncle Charles's wife, who loves to decorate and shop, helped her pick it out. "We looked all over for the perfect one, went to so many places, and I finally found it."

Obaachan is funny this way. She is often flexible about details—she isn't a person who fusses about colors or brands, and most of the time, her main priority is functionality. But on occasion, when she decides she wants or needs something, she knows precisely what she wants, and nothing else will do. She will keep looking until she finds that specific item, that specific shade of blue or gray, that particular material.

I climb onto the corner of the bed and sit down, hanging my legs over the side. There's a large mirror on top of the dresser, right across from the bed, and I see myself in the reflection. I look around the room: another dresser that matches the larger one, stained the same strange, yellowy shade. A nightstand beside the bed. A small bookshelf in the corner of the room, with a few of Obaachan's favorites: *Jane Eyre, Sense and Sensibility*, and a handful of others. Despite her vast reading repertoire, she doesn't own many books. On the opposite side of the room, Obaachan sits at her desk, gazing out the window at the golf course.

"I don't know much about golf," Obaachan says, "but sometimes these old men look so funny when they swing." We watch as a pair of golfers whirl past on their cart. The sun is high in the sky, and the golfers are wearing visors. Obaachan straightens a stack of papers and turns to look at me. "You have more questions for me?" she asks with a look of expectancy. She is all business today.

"Yes," I say with a smile, adjusting my position on the bed. "I always have questions. Are you getting tired of all the interviews?"

"No," she says emphatically, and I believe her.

"Well," I pause to figure out the best way to put it. "I guess I still don't have a sense of how you spent your free time." I realize the irony of the terminology—free time in prison—but don't know how else to say it. "You know, what you did when you weren't working at the mess hall, or taking care of chores. I mean, did you have free time?"

Obaachan frowns, twists her mouth to the side, and says nothing for a moment. What did she do during those years at Heart Mountain—besides work at the mess hall, sweep the apartment, wash and iron clothes? How were those thousands of hours spent? Where were they spent? With whom? Oddly, the memories of everyday life are the most elusive. While she struggles to recall how she spent her time each day, and the names of the neighbors and coworkers she interacted with on a daily basis, my grandmother does remember, often with vivid clarity, special events and specific people who made an impression.

The first winter at Heart Mountain, sometime around when my grandparents married, the authorities had a local fire company come to the camp and flood a concave area to create an ice-skating rink. With the harsh temperatures, the water froze quickly. "I'd never ice-skated before," Obaachan says, remembering, smiling a little. She adjusts her position on the chair. "But I ordered a pair of skates from the Montgomery Ward catalog." In the end, she only skated a handful of times—the temperatures and wind made being outdoors too uncomfortable for her. But for many Heart

Mountain prisoners, ice-skating was a popular means of entertainment during the long winters. "And then there was the Heart Mountain craft show," she says. "Women, farm women who probably all of a sudden had time to do things they were very skilled at, made the most beautiful things." Quilts with perfect patterns of calico prints. Embroidered pillows with intricate designs. Blankets crocheted with brilliant colors of yarn.

Certain people remain in my grandmother's memory as well. In my grandparents' barrack, there was a curious family of four. The daughter was probably close to Obaachan in age, and she was polite, but always quiet, the type of person whose shyness seemed to inhibit her from even looking at people she didn't know. Her brother was a giant. He towered over everyone in camp, and his huge frame moved clumsily through the lines and crowds. His eyes had a sort of vacancy, and his mother was with him at all times, nudging him forward, holding on to his elbow, protecting him. He rarely spoke, but occasionally, he would smile, and when he did, his face would brighten like a warm spring day. This bulky, intimidating young man was really as harmless as an infant.

"And then there was Cowboy Joe," Obaachan says with a giggle, leaning back in her chair. Long before blue jeans were fashionable, this young man wore them every day. Along with his jeans, he sported a tan cowboy hat with a wide brim, and a pair of worn brown-leather cowboy boots. He seemed to rotate his flannel shirts, wearing the red one, then the blue one, every other day. "The only cowboys I'd seen were in movies," Obaachan says. "You know, Westerns. And of course I'd thought there was no such thing as a Japanese cowboy." She wondered where he had lived before the war. Had he been a ranch hand? Had he ridden horses for days, driving cattle across thousands of acres? Or did he simply like the cowboy style of clothing? My grandmother never learned the answers to these questions—she didn't actually ever speak to the young man—but Cowboy Joe was a source of interest and curiosity among the women Obaachan knew, particularly during long and tedious hours on the job.

Another memorable character from camp lived in Obaachan's barrack, just a few doors down. He was very flamboyant and effeminate, powdering his face each morning so that he looked almost like a *geisha*, and always walking with a notable sway in his hips. Before the war, he had been an actor or director in a theatre, and he continued his theatrical work at Heart Mountain. One year, for the big New Year's celebration, he dressed as a woman. He stuffed his dress so that it appeared as though he had enormous breasts, and he wore lots of blush and eye makeup in addition to his usual face powder. Around and around he danced at that party, spinning and laughing as though he was having the time of his life. At the time it was one of the most bizarre events my grandmother had ever seen. She still recalls the experience with a fit of shy laughter.

But of all the interesting and unusual people my grandmother came into contact with at Heart Mountain, perhaps most memorable of all would be the one *hakujin* who had willingly come there as a prisoner. The woman was tall and had shoulder-length blonde hair, and in the sea of shorter, black-haired inmates, she was always easily spotted. Her name was Estelle Ishigo, and after the evacuation from the West Coast was announced, she had decided to go with her Japanese husband.

This woman's choice to marry a Japanese man was in and of itself an act of rebellion and courage. Not only was it taboo to marry outside of your race at the time, it was actually illegal for a *hakujin* woman to marry a Japanese man in California. Their marriage was legally legitimate, so they must have traveled out of state for the ceremony. When Estelle had learned of the evacuation from the West Coast, she had written and asked for permission from the U.S. government to join her husband at the camp, and they allowed her to do so. The stipulation, however, was that she herself would be treated as every other evacuee. She was not to expect any preferential treatment whatsoever, the government informed her.

My grandmother did not know Estelle Ishigo personally, but she would say hello to her when their paths crossed. When I imagine Estelle, I think of her as the type of person my grandmother would have looked up to—despite their very obvious differences—and I think Obaachan respected this incredible woman, who drew and painted and played the violin in the Heart Mountain mandolin band, and whose convictions and devotion to her husband forced her away from her own family and into years of imprisonment.

Of course, during her imprisonment, my grandmother never would have imagined that all four of her children would end up marrying *hakujin*, that almost three decades later, long after every prisoner had left Heart Mountain, long after the rickety wooden barracks had begun to decay, long after my grandparents had moved to the East Coast to start a new life and raise a family, my *hakujin* father, a young man who'd recently returned from a tour in Vietnam, would marry their daughter. His father, my Pap-Pap, a quiet man with steady green eyes who had fought in the Pacific during the war, never expressed any disapproval of the union, at least not that I know of. At Heart Mountain Obaachan would not have imagined that her oldest grandchild would have light brown hair; that all of us would end up not with the dark eyes of our Japanese parent, but with varying shades of hazel and green; that the Japanese in us would, generation by generation, be growing less distinct.

I remember my grandfather explaining to me as a child that because I was not one hundred percent Japanese, it was possible that I would be looked down upon in Japan—I wasn't "pure." I don't believe he said this to upset me, or to express his regret over my parentage. He did, after all, like my father very much. Instead, I think Ojichan wished to compliment my country of birth, a country he loved and believed in. Despite what he had experienced here, America was, for the most part, more tolerant than the Japan of his youth. I'm supposing Ojichan had made that determination about racial "purity" based upon his own experiences in Japan, back in the 1920s, when the country remained suspicious of Western influence. He knew with my green eyes and my hair that was not quite dark enough, I'd immediately be marked as a *hapa*, or person of half-Japanese descent.

Today, this prejudice has changed significantly, and Japan is known for its great interest in American culture, with its brand names and styles. Young people dye their hair lighter; they wear colored contacts to conceal their dark brown eyes, and, alarmingly, they even have surgeries to make the crease in their eyelids more pronounced. In their magazines, it's common to see biracial models, precisely because they exhibit *hakujin* characteristics. In the 1940s, however, in the depressing and segregated corner that was their existence, my grandparents would not have dreamed that such a world could exist.

At her desk, Obaachan takes a sip of water from one of the sepia Honda glasses she and my grandfather have had for decades and wipes her mouth with a napkin.

"With that snake in my courtyard, though, the one I killed, well, at my age, Kimi, I have to just go ahead and do things," Obaachan says, changing the subject after there has been a pause. It becomes clear to me that the killing of the snake is a milestone of sorts, a major accomplishment for her—as I suppose it should be. "You see, I couldn't let my fear keep me from doing what I needed to do. I don't climb up on ladders anymore, and I don't mind asking for help when someone's here visiting, but I can't be calling people, the neighbor or your aunt and uncle, and asking them for help any time something's a little difficult. I need to take care of myself."

This sense of needing to handle things on her own is not a characteristic Obaachan has grown into in old age—it's something gathered over a lifetime, I think—but when did it begin for her? Was it in her teenage years, when, as she herself has told me, the duties of taking care of her mother and the rest of the household chores simply fell upon her shoulders? Was it in her first few months of marriage, when she realized, too late, that my grandfather was so demanding, and that he would not be the source of comfort and support that she'd hoped? Was it when she had children of her own? Or maybe it's something else, one of those events she has chosen not to tell me about.

Chapter 11

THE NEXT AFTERNOON, OBAACHAN STANDS IN HER kitchen, leaning against the white countertop, the Florida heat growing dangerously warm outside, the air conditioning humming softly. In her left hand she holds the periwinkle dish towel I bought her in Stratford and sent from England the spring I studied abroad there. (I think she gets it out each time I visit, maybe the morning I'm to arrive, because each March it's clipped with a clothespin to the handle of her stove, for drying dishes, as though that's where she keeps it, always, in plain view.) The towel is composed of squares with sketches of Shakespeare characters in famous scenes, each from one of his plays: Iago whispering to Othello, Hamlet holding a human skull, three witches hovering over a cauldron, and others.

It's noon. Obaachan has already exercised—an abbreviated walk around the neighborhood, not the two-mile loop she used to do, when I first began visiting her. Around Christmastime, she fell in her bedroom, and since then, she is not as sure on her feet. She now limits her walks to a mile. By this point in the day she has already aired out the house and closed it back up, and watered the plants in her courtyard as well. If I weren't visiting she would spend the afternoon reading at the desk in the corner of her large bedroom, where the window overlooks the golf course, or maybe watching a movie from the library on the portable DVD player my uncle Jay recently bought her. She just bought *Girl with a Pearl Earring* for $5.50 at Walmart, she tells me, which she read and loved as a novel. "In the movie, Colin Firth is the painter," she says with a grin. "You know Colin Firth. 'Mr. Darcy,'" she adds in a British accent, referring to the BBC version of *Pride and Prejudice*.

I sometimes wonder whether my grandmother gets lonely living by herself in Florida. Her days vary little here, and her life is characterized by precision. She goes to few places: the Publix grocery store nearby, the Suntree Public Library down the street, and, on occasion, the Bealls outlet, a discount warehouse with thousands of items that did not sell at the main Bealls store. On Sunday mornings, Obaachan watches a Charles Stanley sermon on television, leaning forward and squinting at the lean, tall figure on the screen, but on most other days, she takes her morning walk and then spends the afternoon at home. Between noon and twelve thirty, she makes lunch, a bowl of *miso* soup with a sliced apple for dessert, or something else light and healthy. In the afternoons, she'll read an article from *Time*, clip a recipe or two from *Real Simple*, do a Sudoku puzzle. And at five thirty, she begins cooking dinner. She watches the evening news on the small, old television set in her dining room while she eats. But she insists she isn't lonely, likes that Emily Brontë line from *Wuthering Heights*: "A sensible man ought to find sufficient company in himself."

Once, when I encouraged her to have some more local contacts in case of an emergency, she shrugged and said, "I have a friend, a Japanese lady, who lives in the next neighborhood over. We both walk in the mornings, so sometimes I see her. She has my number, and I have hers." Her Colombian neighbor, "the gentleman," could also be called upon for help when absolutely necessary. She didn't need any more acquaintances, I inferred from her furrowed brow and pursed lips—or advice from meddling grandchildren.

Obaachan has fostered this same sense of independence in her four children. Even though my grandfather was the one who made all the decisions in the house, the one who controlled the atmosphere and timetable of every day, it was my grandmother, I believe, who possessed the strength to keep the family together through so many transitions and hardships. It was Ojichan who relied on my grandmother to make things happen for him.

At Heart Mountain, one such thing was to have children. The pressure began shortly after their wedding in December of 1942. Obaachan wanted children, she assures me, and in fact, she quickly became obsessed with getting pregnant. Lots of young people got married at Heart Mountain—Obaachan was not the only one to feel the strain of the war when it came to securing a partner—and lots of them were having babies. With so many infants and toddlers coming through the line at the mess hall, Obaachan began to feel ready to have a child of her own, but she felt it took her awhile to get pregnant. It didn't help, I'm sure, that my grandfather was desperate to start a family; he undoubtedly would have been vocal about this desire. Each month Obaachan hoped and prayed that the small red stain would not make its regular appearance, but each month, it showed up. "Not this month," she would have to tell my Ojichan, her eyes lowered, her mouth twisted to the side in disappointment. "I'm sorry."

When my grandmother at last missed a period, two months before their one-year anniversary, she didn't mention it to my grandfather right away. She couldn't bear to get his hopes up and then disappoint him. She studied the calendar posted at the community center, counted out the weeks, and calculated that the baby would probably be born somewhere around her birthday, in July. She felt relieved that she would not have to be concerned about caring for a newborn in the cruel winter months. The drafty room and bitter-cold days would have been difficult: keeping the child warm enough, bathing, cleaning the cloth diapers, and scheduling trips to the restroom whenever someone else could watch the baby would be only a few of the challenges. In July, the weather would be hot and dry, and she would have until September until the snow began—just enough time to get used to motherhood, she thought.

When he heard the news about Obaachan's pregnancy, my grandfather was elated. After spending four years completely alone, with his loved ones on the other side of the Pacific, family had become very important to him. Having a child of his own was something he'd been dreaming about for years. "I'm going to be a father," Ojichan would say, repeating the words over and over when they were in their room or sitting on the small wooden porch at the entryway. He talked about the baby constantly—whether it would be a boy or a girl; good names for a child and whether to choose a Japanese name or an American one; how he hoped his children might one day meet his mother. Although Ojichan's father had passed away by the time the United States entered the war, he always hoped he might see his mother again one day, and now, he would have a grandchild in tow.

Meanwhile, Obaachan suffered from terrible morning sickness. At first, she thought something was wrong. No one had explained to her that it was a common issue. Her mother never talked to her about sex or pregnancy or other private matters of the body, so she assumed the frequent vomiting was a bad sign. Obaachan had no appetite, and she even lost weight in her first trimester. Certain foods and smells—things she had always eaten—would overwhelm her with nausea. Going to the mess hall for the morning meal was always difficult. She was weak because she couldn't hold down anything she ate, and many of the kitchen aromas made her sick.

Obaachan's first visit to the hospital at Heart Mountain helped put her mind at ease. In the small white room, a *hakujin* nurse ordered her to slip into a gown and then returned to check her blood pressure and weight. Her doctor was one of the two *hakujin* doctors hired by the War Relocation Authority to serve the ten thousand internees at Heart Mountain. He looked a little young to be a doctor with his thick blond hair and fleshy red cheeks, but he seemed knowledgeable and confident during the checkup. When he gently pressed his fingers into her abdomen, Obaachan twitched nervously. She still did not look pregnant, and no man besides Ojichan had ever seen her stomach.

"Is everything okay?" she asked as the doctor jotted down a few notes on his clipboard.

The doctor assured her she seemed to be in good shape. "I see here that you told the nurse you're having some morning sickness," he added, reading over Obaachan's file. "You needn't worry about that. Many women have it early in the pregnancy. Give it a few more weeks and I bet you'll be feeling just fine."

Obaachan wondered whether this was true, or if the doctor was simply trying to console her. Surely she could not survive nine months of daily vomiting and consistent waves of nausea or continue to have no appetite and lose weight. In these early months, my grandmother felt so sick that there were moments when she wondered why she had so desperately wanted a baby. But, just as the doctor predicted, by the third month, she no longer had morning sickness, and her pregnancy became much easier.

As soon as Obaachan began feeling better, she became a very conscientious mother-to-be. Although it was difficult to do so because of the limited options at the mess hall, especially in the winter months, when the prisoners could not farm the nearby fields, she tried to eat properly, following the doctor's recommendation to try to eat vegetables and protein as much as possible. She also made herself drink three servings of milk a day, which she knew was important for the baby's growth. At each meal, she sat down after her shift, and sipped milk from a tall, thin mess-hall glass. Realizing that Heart Mountain was not going to be the most idyllic place to raise a child, she wanted to give her baby the best opportunity to be as healthy and strong as possible by taking care of him in the womb.

I can't help wondering how I would have felt about having children if I were in my grandmother's situation. Given the poor living conditions and especially the uncertainty about what the next day would bring, I find it somewhat surprising that she would have wanted to have a child at all. She and her fellow prisoners had no idea whether they would be there for a few more months, or years, or—and most certainly, this terrifying thought must have haunted them in dark moments—forever. Then again, perhaps the idea of raising a child was in some way an attempt at autonomy, a desire to create a better future. I feel just a little bit guilty for questioning my grandparents' strong yearning to start a family. I know I've never faced the hardships and inequalities they have—it's hard to say how I would have acted.

After all, it seems that everyone, both authorities and prisoners, tried to make the best of the situation by creating a sense of longevity at Heart Mountain. The Heart Mountain hospital was sufficiently equipped and staffed. There were also a number of options in terms of entertainment. In addition to the movies that were shown two times a week, there was a community center that hosted activities like art exhibits, featuring work done by some of the prisoners, including paintings and handmade crafts. People created bands that performed concerts. In the summer months, the authorities filled a hole that a group of young men had dug, creating a swimming pool where many prisoners spent the long, hot afternoons, and where children splashed for hours on end. But what would it be like for a child to grow up in a small, dusty room, with no meals ever taken together as a family at a kitchen table, no trips to the grocery store, no family excursions, no memories except what was permitted within that barbed-wire enclosure? Wouldn't it be strange to discuss democracy, the Constitution, and the merits of America?

Aside from that cruel paradox, the education available at Heart Mountain was certainly not ideal. Most people wouldn't really think about their child's education so early, but my grandparents, both of whom were obsessed with it, probably did the minute Obaachan became pregnant. The teachers at Heart Mountain were expected to sign year-long contracts, rather than nine-month ones like their colleagues employed in "regular" school districts. (They were paid $2,000 for twelve months; their peers working outside of the camp were compensated $1,920 for nine. And Wyoming Congressman John J. McIntyre still argued that the Heart Mountain teachers were being overpaid for their services.) Moreover, the student-to-teacher ratio was forty-eight to one in the elementary school and fifty to one in the secondary school.

When the schools opened in October of 1942, classes were held in uninsulated barracks with one dim light that hung from the center of the barrack. Students had no desks, and they were forced to share limited textbooks. In other words, if a high school student had chemistry homework to complete, she would have to return to school in the evening and sign out a book. Hopefully, another student would not have beaten her to it. Chalkboards were made of a simple piece of plywood painted black. By May of 1943, though, a high school building had been constructed, complete with an auditorium, a gymnasium, a home economics room, a machine shop, and a wood shop. The high school students, the Heart Mountain Eagles, even competed with other local teams in athletic events. There was, overall, a great attempt to make life "normal" for the young people at Heart Mountain, which probably helped to put the minds of parents at ease.

I'm not sure when my grandparents' passion for education began—although Obaachan's desire to go to college suggests that it was always important to her—but both of them made it a top priority in our family. Ojichan, concerned that I would not learn to multiply, quizzed me on my times tables when I was in third grade. He would get out his globe, spin it slowly, fingers spread out and pressed to it, and point to various countries to help me get a sense of world geography. Even though he never finished high school because he'd left Japan just shy of seventeen, he read constantly and made an effort to be learning, always, whether it was about nutrition, or gardening, or the stock market. Obaachan has since told me that she still regrets not attending college, and that she did not want to raise her family in the way that her own parents did. The daughters, she would always insist, must have the same educational opportunities as the sons.

Obaachan turns to look out the kitchen window at her grapefruit trees, which are heavy with the full yellow fruit. "After we found out we were having a baby, maybe something clicked in me," she says softly. "It's hard to explain, but all of a sudden I started growing so tired of everything." She shakes her head, folds her hands, and turns to look at me. "I just couldn't wait to get out of there."

It was not so much the rules and the physical limi-
tations of the barbed wire that got to her, or even the
homesickness or brutal Wyoming winters. It was, in my
grandmother's own words, "all those Japanese people"
that began to wear on her. She grew frustrated with the
shikataganai attitude, the swarms of sad faces that made
no effort to change their plight, the sense of hopelessness
that pervaded the camp.

My grandfather, too, began dreaming of life after
Heart Mountain. "I don't think we should return to
California," he announced one day.

Obaachan looked up from her position on her cot.
She was sewing herself a smock for later in the pregnancy, one of her two maternity shirts. She'd bought
the fabric, a soft yellow calico cotton, at the Heart
Mountain dry-goods store.

"Because it won't be the same, you know," my
grandfather continued. "People won't want us there.
They never have. And if you thought it was bad before,
imagine how it will be when the war ends. Plus," he
added, pausing, "we need to go out on our own. Start
life on our own terms, the two of us."

Obaachan said nothing. While she desperately
longed to return to her old home and old life, to the
way things were—the house on Pico Street with Papa's
camellias, the buzz of shoppers, and the thick smell of
shoyu in Little Tokyo—part of her must have realized

that the life she had known before the war would never return. Ojichan was right. It was probably best to leave that life behind. To move on. She wondered where the rest of her family would end up. Would her parents return to Los Angeles? Or would they seek a fresh start as well? What about her sister, brother-in-law, and nephew? Where would they go? And what about her brothers, both of whom had enlisted? She wondered about her family, even though she had already begun to lose touch with them. She had seen her older brother a few times—he worked as a pharmacist in a German POW camp in Indiana and would come to Heart Mountain whenever he had leave—but she had not seen her younger brother or her sister since the spring of 1942.

"We should be farmers," Ojichan continued, his voice determined. "Like the book says. All you need is five acres, and you can grow enough to sustain yourself. You trade the things you grow for other things you might need, like meat. Imagine being completely independent—not needing anyone! No government telling you what to do or where to go, no people charging too much at the store. It would just be us, our family," he said, looking at Obaachan, studying her face.

My grandfather was referring to a book he had recently borrowed from the Heart Mountain library: *Five Acres and Independence*. Written in 1935, this classic back-to-the-land how-to is still in print today. How enticing that title would have been to them! On my grandfather's insistence, Obaachan read it when he was finished. The book talked about how with five acres and a careful plan, it was possible to be self-sufficient. Both of them found it inspiring, and my grandfather, who was easily caught up in exciting schemes, was especially enthralled.

"As soon as the war ends and we can get out of here, we'll take out a loan and buy property. Somewhere in the Midwest, maybe. Good farming country there. And I think people won't be so against the Japanese. They might be more open to having us as their neighbors. It's gotta be better than the West Coast. I'm sure of that."

Obaachan did not wish to deter his enthusiasm, and she'd already learned not to disagree with her husband, so she simply raised her eyebrows in an approving way, smiled, and returned to her sewing. At the back of her mind, she probably considered the many pitfalls in my grandfather's plan. First, would they ever be allowed to leave Heart Mountain? Wasn't he getting ahead of himself? And besides, if they were permitted to leave, would they be able to own property? Would there be a day when *hakujin* people didn't mind having Japanese neighbors? Or would they always be eyed with suspicion and disapproval? She suppressed the urge to speak of these things. There was no point in smothering

Ojichan's dream if it helped him get through the long days in their prison, nor was there any use in spoiling his good mood. Since learning that a baby was on the way, he had been especially cheerful and helpful. It was springtime, and the baby would be arriving soon. Obaachan needed my grandfather to be in the best of spirits for the months ahead.

"My pregnancy was going along smoothly, but then, in May, I had a, well—" Obaachan pauses, watching the branches of the grapefruit tree lift and sway as the afternoon breeze picks up. "A close call, I guess you could say."

She was trying to brew Ojichan a cup of tea. She grabbed the copper kettle in their apartment and waddled toward the laundry room down the block, which always had boiling water available. Inside, a woman she recognized but did not know glanced at Obaachan's swelling stomach and asked how far along she was.

"Eight weeks left," she told the woman, smiling. My grandmother only gained about twenty pounds with each of her four pregnancies, so she would not have looked all that big, even in her third trimester.

As Obaachan walked slowly back to her apartment, the boiling kettle in hand, she looked ahead, at the mountain, rising up from the plain, sharp and almost pretty with just a little bit of snow left near its peak.

After eight months of winter, Obaachan could finally sense spring in the air, in the meadowlarks that flitted about the barracks and the green stems of tulips that were just beginning to emerge from the ground. The sun felt warm on her face and her bare arms, and she took a deep breath, content.

And then, without warning, she felt a searing pain ripple through her body, burning her skin, the pain so sharp she could barely breathe, her legs weakening, and then her body falling toward the ground. Everything went black.

Chapter 12

WHEN OBAACHAN WOKE UP FROM BLACKING OUT THAT afternoon in May of 1944, it took her a few moments to realize where she was. A metal cart with a stack of folded towels and thin, shiny instruments. A tall, white shelf stocked with glass mason jars and brown medicine bottles. The low hum of people bustling about and exchanging words. As her eyes adjusted to the brightness, she figured out that she was in the Heart Mountain hospital. Beside her, Ojichan sat in a sloped wooden chair, leaning forward nervously, and as soon as she stirred, he took hold of her hand and forced a smile. Her father stood in the corner, his brown hands folded at his waist, holding his fedora hat, his head lowered.

"What happened?" Obaachan asked, her voice hoarse. Her hand moved instinctively toward her abdomen. "What's going on?" She sat up in her bed.

"Shhh," my grandfather cooed. "Don't try to get up. Be still. The boiling water from the tea, it spilled all over you on your way home. Nobody saw it happen, so we don't know if you tripped or what happened." He paused and glanced at his father-in-law. "Do you remember?"

She shook her head and began to cry. "The baby?"

My grandfather let go of her hand and looked away. "They can't be sure yet."

The doctor, the same *hakujin* man who'd given my grandmother her initial checkup months earlier and reassured her that her pregnancy was progressing nicely, tapped lightly on the open door and walked in with his clipboard. Obaachan wiped her eyes with her sleeve and looked at him, nervously fiddling with the sheets. The doctor glanced at my grandfather, trying to assess whether he had told Obaachan about the baby's status.

"We'll need a day or two," he said, tucking his clipboard beneath his arm and shuffling his feet. "You went through a good deal of trauma, so it's just hard to determine the baby's status right now. We'll know in a few days whether you'll be able to carry to full term." Although she cannot recall what happened exactly, my grandmother does know that somehow, after she blacked out, she had spilled the kettle of boiling water all over the front of herself that afternoon in May—her abdomen and legs were badly burned.

Today, so many decades later and with four healthy grown children, my grandmother can look back on this event and describe it as though it were just another everyday occurrence, a mere bump in the road during that era of her life. She admits that it was frightening, and that she was nervous about the outcome, but the incident must have been much worse than she lets on. Considering her months of trying to become pregnant, and considering my grandfather's obsession with having children, I imagine Obaachan must have felt an enormous amount of anxiety. Those days in the small Heart Mountain hospital must have dragged on with unbearable slowness for both of my grandparents. With every sound of footsteps in the hallway, Obaachan would have looked toward the door, waiting for the doctor, hoping he would arrive in the doorway, smiling, his clipboard in hand, bringing good news. Although Ojichan said nothing about the boiling water during my grandmother's time in the hospital, she knew even then how he felt about the duties of a mother. A part of him must have held her responsible for the accident. In the years to come, he would make clear to her the seriousness of her role as the mother of his children: "You alone are responsible for our children's safety. It's your fault if something happens to them," he would remind her, long after they'd left Heart Mountain and had more children.

While Obaachan would later take on that role of keeping the children safe, my grandfather would become the family disciplinarian. On more than one occasion, my mother has described Ojichan's strict rules, his fiery temper—and his firm belief in that biblical proverb about sparing the rod and spoiling the children. My mother, outspoken, intense, and impulsive, took after Ojichan in terms of temperament, which frequently led to encounters with my grandfather's infamous black-leather belt. Once, walking the family dog, my mother witnessed her older sister flirting with a neighbor boy and crying out for help. My mother, not realizing that her sister was playing around, ran to her aid and began thrashing the young man with the metal dog chain until she realized what was going on. This event resulted in both girls being punished with the belt.

Unlike Obaachan, who determined early on that there was no point in arguing with my grandfather and that it was unwise to anger him, my mother had no qualms about voicing her opinion. She refused to let my grandfather get the last word in during any confrontation, which only angered Ojichan more. "If you'd just learn to keep your mouth shut," her sister told her, "you'd be punished much less." But my mother couldn't help herself. She'd argue and complain, insist that she had not been wrong, sass my grandfather, even when his belt was in his hand. My brother and I never saw this side of my grandfather—he was not allowed to discipline us—but in the moments we witnessed flashes of his temper, we understood not to anger him.

After a few long days, the blond doctor showed up again at my grandmother's hospital room that May of 1944. He held the stethoscope to Obaachan's abdomen, pressed his fingertips into various places one more time, examined the purple streaks and blisters on her stomach and legs. He smiled. "We're letting you go home," he said. "The baby seems to be doing just fine."

Overwhelmed with relief, Obaachan buried her face in my grandfather's shoulder. Papa, who had stayed at the hospital as much as his duties permitted him, nodded, relieved as well, and without a word, slipped on his fedora hat and walked home to tell his wife.

In Florida, Obaachan and I are watching the Oscars in the front bedroom of her house. There's a bed here, but the mattress is old and uncomfortable and moans and veers from side to side when someone sits on it. There's a television (a new flat screen, which my uncle Jay, the most technologically inclined one in the family, purchased for her on his last visit), and a wicker table with a glass top where Obaachan sometimes sits and works through Sudoku puzzles in the afternoons. There's also a tall bookshelf that almost reaches the ceiling, and it's full of family photographs and an assortment of hard-back books purchased from the local library's annual spring sale.

I'm sprawled out on the bed, a stack of lumpy down pillows stacked behind my back, and a large stainless-steel bowl of popcorn propped between my knees. Earlier in the evening, we made the popcorn on the stovetop, according to Obaachan's directions. Measure three tablespoons of canola oil into a saucepan over medium-high heat. Toss in two kernels, and when they pop, you know the oil is hot. Then add in a third of a cup of popcorn, replace the lid, and shake the pan to let the steam out until the popping ceases. Immediately remove the pan from the burner. Divide the popcorn; add sea salt, no butter.

In the front bedroom Obaachan is seated on a wooden chair with a thin, worn blue pad, where she always sits for movies. Tonight, she has seen more of the nominated films than I have and knows the predicted winners according to the local newspaper. Compared to her, I haven't been following movies too well this year.

"Don't talk to me about George Clooney," she says, drawing out the double-O in his last name, wrinkling her nose when he steps on screen in a sleek black tuxedo. Her slight Japanese accent is noticeable when she says his name. "I can't stand him."

Surprised, I ask her why. "Isn't he sort of that old Hollywood type of guy from your generation?"

"I just don't like to watch him." She shrugs. "I don't know. I just don't like his face. And I never have, not even when he was on *ER*."

We watch in silence for a few moments, gaping at the expensive gowns and fancy suits, and then she begins asking me about various Hollywood figures. She likes Cate Blanchett and Nicole Kidman, disapproves of Angelina Jolie, except for the fact that she gives a lot to charity. She reminds me that she named my mother after Rosalind Russell, a woman my grandmother admired for playing strong, gutsy characters who knew how to stand up for themselves.

When the Three 6 Mafia arrives on stage to sing "It's Hard out Here for a Pimp," Obaachan gets up from her wooden chair near the door and leaves. I listen as her slippers shuffle across the carpet and hear her bedroom door close softly behind her. She never comes back, and I'm left to wonder what happened. I'd been holding the remote—should I have changed the channel? Did the song offend her?

The next morning, at breakfast, she explains her exit, shaking her head with a look of disgust. "I can't stand rap music. Maybe it's because I'm old. You know, things are just too overwhelming, too loud." A few years earlier, I'd taken her to a nearby movie theatre in Florida to see *Chicago*—which I thought she'd like, since it was a film about "her" time—and she'd hated it. Too much flash, too much flesh.

"Do you like rap music, Kimi?"

I tell her I don't mind some of it, on occasion.

"I read about one guy, a rapper, in *Time*." She pauses, silently forming letters with her lips. "Kona? Keen? I can't remember. His name started with a K."

"Kanye West?"

Her face lights up. "That's him. You know him? Do you listen to him?"

I laugh then, the whole conversation striking me as odd and fascinating. My mother is wildly out of touch with pop culture, and proud of it, I think, and yet my grandmother, in her eighties, has read about Kanye West. I tell her I'm impressed, and she shrugs. "I read, watch the news. Even though I'm old, I don't have to be completely out of the loop," she says with a smile.

At Heart Mountain, all new mothers received a kit packed with various items a newborn might need. In each kit were cloth diapers; a little vest; flannel *kimonos*; pads to prevent soiling the baby's sheets; soakers, which were crocheted or knitted and used to put over the diapers; and two gowns. A group of Quaker women from Philadelphia made all of these items, packed them up, and shipped them to the internment camps across the country. Quakers, who as a whole protested the imprisonment of Japanese Americans, voiced their opposition prior to removal, but their opinions were drowned out by more powerful forces, so they did what they could to help. When I contact the Quaker Information Center in Philadelphia, I have no luck in tracking down more information about these women and the care packages they sent to Heart Mountain. Perhaps it was the American Friends Service Committee who oversaw this project, or a Friends school, or even a local congregation—we can find no record of the event.

Still, my grandmother distinctly remembers receiving that package from the Quakers. As she opened the kit and took out the clean, pastel-colored items, all of which were neatly folded and placed into a basket, she fell silent. Having just returned from her scare at the hospital, and still in a lot of pain from the burns, seeing the small green vest and feeling the soft *kimonos* moved her. She had done enough sewing and crocheting to understand just how much time and effort had gone into preparing the package, and a feeling of gratitude overwhelmed her.

"Whenever I felt myself getting angry about all that had happened to us, or sad about losing our home on Pico Street, or when I was frustrated by all the dust and the cold weather, I thought about those women. About their generosity to us, even though they were from the East Coast and wouldn't have known any of us."

After all, even her own neighbors back in Los Angeles—people her family had known for decades—had abandoned them after Pearl Harbor, refusing to offer help with packing up or storing items. My grandmother pictured those Quaker women bringing their handmade items to the meeting house and tenderly organizing them into kits, and in that image of kindness and compassion, she found comfort. There were people outside their barbed-wire prison who had not forgotten about them, who did not see them as the cruel, vicious race of enemies described in the papers and in the newsreels, but as human beings, caught up in forces beyond their control.

"I should have thanked them," Obaachan says, shaking her head, frustrated with herself. "There are things I should have done. I see them now, too late. I should have sent a letter or something. To let them know what it meant to me. When you're older, you look back and you realize there are people who lifted you up, who helped you."

But at the time she was very distracted, not only by the coming of her baby, but by her mother's health, which continued to decline. Toward the end of Obaachan's pregnancy, her mother was taken to the Heart Mountain hospital, where she would remain for months.

"We always knew," Obaachan says softly, folding her hands and placing them on the blue cloth placemats on the dining-room table. She straightens out a wrinkle in the tablecloth. "We knew that she would not live for long, even from the beginning, back when I was just a teenager. The doctors told us. It was only a matter of time."

Shortly before Obaachan's due date in July, my grandfather decided to head to Montana with a work crew. This decision seems slightly out of character for him, as he had not done this before, and it also strikes me as odd, given his anticipation about becoming a parent. Wouldn't he want to be there for the baby's arrival?

"We could use the extra money," he explained when he came home and told my grandmother he'd signed up for a team that was leaving the next day. "For the baby."

Work crews frequently left Heart Mountain to pick the sugar beets and beans that grew in Montana, Wyoming, and Nebraska. Prior to the establishment of the Heart Mountain camp, there had been a severe labor shortage in all three of those states. While many Wyoming residents initially opposed the construction of the camp, farmers did realize the potential labor that could come out of this new population. By the time my grandparents arrived in 1942, farmers were filing requests with the Wyoming government to obtain workers from Heart Mountain, inundating their senator with telegrams begging for help.

The process, however, was not all that simple. First, agreements had to be reached among the WRA heads Milton Eisenhower, Dillon S. Meyer, and especially Governor Nels Smith, who wanted assurance that the Japanese would be promptly returned to the camp after their emergency work was done. The good people of Wyoming, he explained, did not under any circumstances want the Japanese setting up permanent residence in their state. He didn't agree to work releases until he was satisfied that wouldn't happen. To further complicate matters, the sixty-three percent of the prisoners at Heart Mountain who were American citizens could not be forced to work. The remaining thirty-seven percent were not legally allowed to become citizens—Obaachan's parents, for instance, would never be permitted citizenship—and could not be forced to work either. It was necessary then to ensure that all those who worked outside of the camp did so voluntarily, and were paid well for their efforts. It was also necessary for area politicians to attempt to distribute the workers evenly, according to acreage farmed. Wyoming farmers tended to resent this arrangement—why should they have to share the workers with Montana and Nebraska?—but in the end they were forced to accept the stipulations.

While many young men from Heart Mountain did end up taking this opportunity to earn additional cash, it did have its drawbacks, the primary one being that there was never a set return date, and there was no way to get in touch with someone once they'd left.

Still, Obaachan didn't argue with my grandfather over his decision to go to Montana. She knew better than to question his judgment, and, besides, he promised to be back in time for her due date. The two of them arranged for Obaachan's Papa to check in on her regularly, just to make sure everything was all right. Because his apartment was on the same block, just across the dirt street that separated the rows of barracks, he could easily stop by several times a day.

As fate would have it, Obaachan's water broke a few days after my grandfather left, one warm July afternoon, two weeks before her due date. She was at home in the apartment, in between shifts at the mess hall. She had Papa request an ambulance, and shortly thereafter, one pulled up in front of her apartment. Two men helped her struggle into the back of the ambulance and then drove her the short distance to the hospital.

Obaachan smiles as she recalls this memory. "I knew absolutely nothing about labor," she tells me—her mother had not prepared her with a single word of explanation or warning—"so I wasn't the least bit afraid. I'd read an article in a newspaper that told of how a baby had been miraculously born in a car on the way to the hospital, and once I'd heard about how a mother had given birth in a department store. And based on those stories, I guess I thought that when the time came, the baby just sort of slipped out."

My grandmother's naïveté about the realities of labor shocks me—surely she didn't really think a baby "slipped out" when it was ready—and yet my shock is, I realize, just another sign of how vastly different the worlds we grew up in were. Obaachan had no clue what to expect on her wedding night, or how to track her cycle when she wanted to get pregnant, or even what she was getting herself into when she decided to have a baby.

I had my first sex-ed class at Alfarata Elementary in the fourth grade. The teacher split us up according to our gender, and we watched a video on how babies are made, what to expect when your first period arrived, and how to use maxipads and tampons. My grandmother, on the other hand, lived in a world where sex was not seen or discussed, where schools wouldn't have dreamed of offering classes on sex education, and where mothers (at least *her* mother) did not give the opportunity to ask questions about menstruation or childbirth. A world in which, if a teenager got pregnant out of wedlock, she might be so ashamed that she'd give birth and leave the baby in a Dumpster—as one young girl did at Heart Mountain.

Two days after Obaachan's labor began, things really started. "They should've sent me home," Obaachan tells me. "They should've told me to go home and call for an ambulance when the labor pains grew stronger. Looking back, I think that's what would've been best for everyone involved."

Instead, she sat around at the hospital for two days, wandering the halls, waiting impatiently for the baby to make its appearance. When the real labor finally began, the pain was so intense and awful that she thought something must be wrong.

"I want to die!" she screamed. "Please! Just let me die! I want to die! Please!" Obaachan recreates the scene for me in her dining room, squinting her eyes, scrunching her face. (I still have trouble imagining her actually screaming that she wanted to die, but I don't interrupt.) "And then a nurse told me, 'Snap out of it, young lady!' She told me I'd better start pushing because the baby was ready to come out, and I'd be better off helping it instead of bawling around." Obaachan looks at me. "She was a tough lady, that nurse," she says, her eyebrows raised, her mouth in a half smile. So Obaachan pushed. And pushed some more. "I was so exhausted," she says, "but every time I wanted to give up, that unsympathetic nurse would glare at me and tell me to keep pushing."

As my grandmother relates this story, she doesn't mention my grandfather's absence. She says nothing of how she was alone in that small delivery room, how in addition to her ignorance about what giving birth would be like, her husband was hundreds of miles north, not knowing she was in labor, picking sugar beets, no doubt making friends and telling stories from San Francisco or his home of Iwakuni on the Inland Sea. In the hallway outside the hospital room, Papa waited. He had been there off and on over the previous two days, when he could be, between caring for his wife and tending to his own daily chores. With only a thin wall separating him from Obaachan, he must have heard her screams.

At last she heard the cry of a baby, that pitiful, heartbreaking sound that only newborns can make. She stretched her neck to see. The formerly severe nurse had a wide smile on her face. Now that the work was over, she transformed into a different person. "Congratulations!" she said cheerfully. "You're a mother. You now have a son."

Although she didn't realize it right away, it turned out that my grandmother gave birth on her own twenty-third birthday, in July of 1944. Her father reminded her when he came in to visit later that evening. Oddly, while my grandmother was in labor, Operation Valkyrie, a failed attempt by the German Resistance to assassinate Hitler—the fourth one that year—was occurring on the other side of the world. With that failure, the German

Resistance nearly crumbled, and Hitler's army would continue fighting for almost another year.

"Happy birthday," Obaachan's Papa said with a smile. He did not reach out to touch her, no squeeze of the hand, no reassuring hug, but he did hold the baby. On that day, as Papa held the little boy, he must have thought of his other grandson, Obaachan's sister's child, whom he'd seen only as a newborn, and only for a few days, right before the evacuation. By now, he was over two years old, likely babbling, certainly running and getting into things, testing his parents. What did he look like? What words did he know? Was he learning to speak both Japanese and English? Papa would not have recognized him if he saw him—he had no photographs of the boy—so he could only wonder about his features and size. What he knew of his grandson would have been compiled from the letters that came each month from Obaachan's sister.

"How are you feeling?" Papa asked. "Do you need anything?"

"Tired. Completely exhausted," Obaachan answered, adding that, no, she did not need anything.

"It was a long labor," he said, looking down, obviously uncomfortable with the topic.

"Did you tell Mama that she has a grandson?"

"Oh, yes." Mama couldn't wait to meet him, Papa assured her. But it would be best to wait awhile before arranging a meeting, at least until Obaachan was out of the hospital.

Obaachan noted the look of concern on his face. "Is something wrong?"

"No, no. She's just tired, I believe. She wanted to come to visit you, but I told her she must wait until you can bring the baby to her instead. It's too much for her to come here. She can't overdo things."

"I'll bring him as soon as I can. Tell her I'll bring him soon."

"I'll be sure to let her know. I'll leave you to rest now," Papa said. He nodded slightly, put on his fedora hat, and smiled. "I'll come back in the morning, after I get your mother's breakfast and have my own. Good night." He walked out the door, the baby went off with a nurse to the nursery ward, and Obaachan fell asleep.

My Ojichan did not return for several more days, and since my grandparents had not determined a name for their child, the boy remained nameless until my grandfather came back to Heart Mountain.

"We'd talked about it, but we hadn't come up with a name," Obaachan explains. "And I didn't want to name him without your grandfather." So she waited. She tried to adjust to the baby's frequent feedings, tried not to be consumed by the many questions that raced through her mind. When was her husband coming home? What kind of future might her son have? Would he remain at Heart Mountain for years? Would he have the chance for a "normal" childhood?

How strange, overwhelming, and disillusioning my grandmother's first experience with childbirth must have been. Not only was she shocked to discover how intensely painful labor could be, but even after she'd given birth, she was alone. Her mother was too ill to visit; her child had no name. And she would have known that my Ojichan had no idea that they had a son. She must have felt the miles and miles of rough Wyoming and Montana terrain that separated them. She must have wondered where he was.

At last Ojichan returned. Papa, having gotten wind of the returning work crew, had been waiting at the entrance to Heart Mountain to tell him the news. Ojichan rushed home, went to the bathrooms to shower and shave, and arrived in my grandmother's hospital room fresh and clean, his curly hair still wet and his cheeks smelling of aftershave. He never would've gone straight to the hospital without cleaning up—for Ojichan, with his obsession with hygiene and appearance, to see his child for the first time in a state of filth not only would have been unsanitary, but a disgrace. So there he was, days after my grandmother had given birth, holding his new baby boy, pressing him against his chest, and smiling. He had waited so long for such a moment.

"Our son," he whispered, looking at the small face and mess of black hair. He studied the baby's features and was silent for a moment. "Charles," he said decidedly, looking up at her with a slow smile. "We will call him Charles." He pressed his lips to the boy's forehead and beamed.

Although their last name was clearly identifiable as Japanese, my grandparents did not give any of their children Japanese first names. I think of Obaachan's story from her adolescence, how she made up a fake name for herself when filling out forms for free makeup and toiletries because her real name "sounded too Japanese." My grandfather had adopted an "American" name himself; no one knew him by the name his family had given him, but by the name he'd chosen in San Francisco. Considering the importance that Japanese families place on naming their children—and choosing the right characters for those names—the decision to break with that tradition must have been somewhat difficult.

Then again, perhaps it is not so surprising that my grandparents decided against Japanese names. Perhaps they saw American first names as a gesture toward showing their patriotism. Perhaps it was a way to protect their children a bit from the prejudice they would undoubtedly face, regardless of what their names were.

"Here," Ojichan said, placing a small box into my grandmother's hand. "I got you this in Montana."

"Oh," Obaachan said, surprised. She reached out her weakened arm. "What is it? You shouldn't have bought me anything. I thought we were saving money for the baby . . ." As soon as she said the words, she knew she shouldn't have done so. A flash of anger flickered like a shadow across my grandfather's face. She quickly took the box in her hand. Ojichan was not fond of receiving advice, particularly of the financial sort.

"Just open it," he said with a forced smile, one that failed to mask the initial emotion. "It's for your birthday."

Obaachan opened the box and gasped. Inside were a necklace and matching ring. They were very unusual: each had an ivory image with brown coloring that reminded her of the silhouette of tall grass along a river. The pendant hung on a delicate gold chain, and the ring was gold, too.

"They're beautiful," she murmured. "Thank you."

She liked the gift very much, and it had been a long time since she had received any type of present. Since my grandfather had not given Obaachan a wedding ring, the necklace and ring would have been the first jewelry she ever received from him. And the set certainly was lovely. But this was the kind of gift that was both touching and frustrating. It appeared to be an expensive purchase, and although Obaachan appreciated her husband's thoughtfulness, her practical side thought that a frivolous set of jewelry was not as important as having some money to help cover the expenses of a new child, especially since she would now be working less at the mess hall. It was also money that could have been saved, should they ever have the opportunity to leave Heart Mountain and start over. The jewelry, on the other hand, would not be of much use. She cringed when she thought of the waste.

Ojichan never did say a word about the money he was supposed to have earned in Montana; he just brought home a few gifts for my grandmother and the baby. She didn't dare ask whether anything had happened to it, or to him. And rather than worry about it, she made up her mind to focus on the present, to take a mental photograph of those first few moments of her life as part of a "real" family, and to imprint the image into a space in her memory where it would not be swallowed up by so many hardships.

Chapter 13

It's September, and although summer should be over here in Pennsylvania, it's hot and humid, we've still had no frost, and the snapdragons at the front of my parents' brick home remain in full bloom, their pinks and yellows tangled. I'm visiting for the weekend, standing at the island in their kitchen, looking over a large blue colander that can barely contain its mound of tomatoes so ripe their skin is bursting. My mother is scalding some of these tomatoes for canning, cooking them just long enough to make the skin come loose. My father has about sixty plants each year, much more than the two of them can ever eat—some primordial need to produce as much food as possible, I think—which means my mother spends late summer and early fall preserving everything she can. She looks up from her vat of boiling water, the steam lifting in a heavy white cloud, her face hot and tired, and says nonchalantly, easily, as if the words have no weight: "Your grandmother's moving."

I drop the tomato I've been holding back into the colander.

"Your aunt and uncle, they're selling the house, and, well, she'll be living somewhere else," she continues.

"What do you mean she's moving? What do you mean they're selling the house?" I say, my tone just a little too strained to hide.

My mother seems surprised, confused by my strong reaction. Twenty years ago, my aunt and her husband purchased the house in Florida and generously allowed my grandparents to live there, free of charge. When my Ojichan passed away, my grandmother remained in the house. My aunt and uncle have never lived in Florida and never intended to; they own homes in Hawaii and Colorado and live in Alaska. Since they've never been short on money, I don't understand why they're selling Obaachan's home—why she has to move. At her age, I fear, packing up and relocating will be a great strain.

"They're downsizing," my mother says with a shrug. "The insurance, what with all the hurricanes . . . it's just not possible for them to keep the place in Florida." She studies my face. "They've put the house in Honolulu on the market as well. They want to simplify."

I frown. Is there something else going on that my mother's just not telling me? Can't something be done to avoid this? Might the rest of the family pitch in to cover expenses? But I know better than to voice my concerns to my mother. She possesses a strange, unrelenting forgiveness toward her sister's actions—Charlotte can do no wrong in her eyes—and if I push her, she'll let me know, as she has before, that I rank below my aunt in her hierarchy of favorites. Deciding to keep my mouth shut, I shuffle outside to the deck at the back of the house and close the glass door behind me.

My father is seated on a white plastic chair, reading a Terry C. Johnston Western, his feet propped up on another white chair, a mug of beer on the table beside him. He looks up, moves his feet as an invitation to join him, and takes off his reading glasses. He never needed glasses until recently, and he still feels embarrassed about wearing them in front of people, even though I think they look distinguished and have told him so.

"Did Mom tell you about Obaachan?" I say, flinging myself into the chair and slumping. "About her house?" (I'm aware that it's not really her house, which is precisely the problem—and yet it *is* her house, which is the point.)

He nods, taking a sip of beer, looking at me, his eyes blue and earnest in the September sunlight. He knows what's on my mind, understands that I'm concerned about Obaachan. He leans back in his chair and places his book on the table, still says nothing. The breeze picks up and the sea of poppies beside the deck sways, their furry stems lifting.

"I mean, Mom doesn't even seem concerned— she doesn't even seem *aware* of what this means for Obaachan. She told me like it was good news or something. Where's Obaachan going to go? What's she going to do? She's eighty-six. It's her *home*."

My father shakes his head and looks down. "I stay out of it," he says with a shrug. It's not his business, not his mother, not his sister, not his family. He understands my mother and her siblings are not interested in how he perceives the situation. (My guess is that he, too, knows where he stands in the hierarchy.) "But it's a shame to see her . . . displaced . . . again," he adds, folding his hands in his lap.

"Yes. Displaced is the word, exactly."

At Heart Mountain, my grandparents struggled to adjust to life with a newborn in that small, dingy room. After a twelve-day stint in the hospital, Obaachan headed home to Block 17. With those thin walls that didn't reach the ceiling, my grandmother must have cringed every time the small boy cried—everyone else in the barrack would have heard it, would have woken up with each feeding and discomfort, as she had, with all the other children who shared their building. My grandmother has always been extraordinarily sensitive to how her actions are perceived by others. She tries her best not to inconvenience or bother people. Once, she told me that people don't like it when old folks run their errands in the evenings. "Old people should go out during the day, so that working people aren't held up," she explained. "We're too slow." At least that's what she had read in a series of editorials in the local newspaper. And after learning that she might be disturbing the routines of some of her fellow Floridians, she made sure that she ran all of her errands during the workday hours. In the close quarters at Heart Mountain, however, there was no such flexibility to accommodate the desires of others. Obaachan simply had to do the best she could.

In her weak condition, Obaachan's mother would not have been able to help with little Charles. On occasion, Obaachan took him to visit her mother, sometimes in her apartment, sometimes in the hospital. Mama certainly would have appreciated seeing her grandson, even though she couldn't interact much. "She was in and out of the hospital at Heart Mountain," Obaachan has told me. "She would be there for a few days, or a couple of weeks, and then she would be sent home for awhile. But as time passed, she was in the hospital more and more."

However, to my grandmother's surprise—and, I must admit, to my own—Ojichan was very hands-on and helpful with the baby. Although I understood as a kid that my grandfather loved children, playing with them is certainly different from helping to care for them. Plus, in a time when family roles were strictly delineated, when men were not expected to help with children or house upkeep, Ojichan changed diapers, walked the baby around the room when he was fussy, and doted on his every move. Years later, when my aunt, mother, and uncle came along, Ojichan played with them, romping around on the floor, just as he did with us grandchildren. Before he became ill with pulmonary fibrosis, Ojichan was always the fun grandfather—the one who took my brother fishing, walked the exercise trails with us, and quizzed us on our times tables. We adored him and knew we could always count on him to transform a boring afternoon into an adventure.

As his illness grew more and more debilitating, his tolerance for our antics waned a bit. By the time I turned thirteen, his jovial manner had changed. "Open the window and turn on the fan," he commanded my brother when he used the bathroom. "Let it run for fifteen minutes. I need the cleanest air possible." In his final years, Ojichan spent most of his time in the tan recliner my grandmother had bought for him, his oxygen tank constantly at his side, the plastic tubes hanging from his nostrils. His face, once handsome and lively, swelled to almost twice its original size. Still, even in those years when he was dying, his hair remained dark, thick, and wavy.

When he passed away, I was on a weekend retreat with a school program, and my mother called to tell me that she was flying to Florida to be with her family and to toss my grandfather's ashes into the Atlantic. My brother and I were not asked to go. I felt little emotion then, with my sixteen-year-old view of the world and its giving and taking. "He was old," I said to myself. (He was actually only seventy-five, so he wasn't that old, really.) "And they all knew he was sick." Surely my mother and her family were not so naïve as to think he might miraculously recover from the pulmonary fibrosis. After all, he'd lived for almost two years beyond what the doctors had predicted.

As a teenager I didn't see my grandfather's death from my mother's perspective, as one losing a father, or from Obaachan's perspective, as a woman losing her husband of over fifty years. Even though my grandfather had moments when he must have been nearly intoler- able as a spouse—he was demanding, particular, and sometimes severe—he was still very much a part of my grandmother's existence. Having married so young, and having spent their first years as a couple imprisoned, they shared a deep bond, one that could only be formed after experiencing five decades together. Neither one seemed to believe in having friends. They were friendly toward their neighbors, said hello if they passed on the street, knew people's names on their block, but never arranged times to meet for dinner, go out for a round of golf, play bridge, or anything like that. The two of them were one another's primary companions. When they retired to Florida, they drove to a nearby fitness trail early each morning, before the weather grew too hot, and exercised together. They kept track of their progress on a chart on a small clipboard: their balance abilities, how long they could hang on the metal bar, how far they walked.

In those early years in Florida, before Ojichan got sick, my brother, mom, and I joined my grandparents on these morning trips when we visited. What I remember most distinctly is their persistent warnings about the deadly fire ants. "Don't go anywhere near those mounds," my grandfather warned, pointing to one of the tiny hills the fire ants had built. He was referring to the red fire ants that were introduced to the state from Brazil. Nonnative species, the ants both sting and bite, and they are notoriously aggressive. Aware of my brother's deep curiosity about insects, Ojichan worked to instill a strong fear of the ants in both of us. "They'll attack you," he warned. "The whole colony. They'll cover you and they can kill you." This was of course an exaggeration, an example of my grandfather's flare for the dramatic, but at the time I was terrified. Having been stung by hornets at the age of three, I had no desire to have a run-in with the stinging and biting red ants, and made sure to keep myself—and my little brother—away from them. Even as an adult, I'm careful not to make the mistake of stepping into a colony of those ants.

At Heart Mountain, my grandmother found herself growing restless in that tiny room.

"I couldn't stand it any longer," she has told me many times, with the same look of frustration, her eyes squinting, her mouth pursed in disgust. "I just couldn't wait to get out of there."

Despite her parents' many lessons on seeing the good in every situation, after two years in Wyoming, Obaachan could no longer force herself to believe that those good things were enough. When she imagined her son spending his childhood at Heart Mountain, going to school with all the other war babies, graduating, and then finding some menial work around camp, as my grandfather and Obaachan's Papa had been forced to do—when she pictured him living forever inside barbed wire, she shuddered. She wanted her son to have the opportunity to walk the streets of a town somewhere, to have meals at a kitchen table with family rather than in a mess hall crammed with strangers. She wanted him to go to a real school where there were not only Japanese students who had grown up in an internment camp. She hoped that he might know what it was like to buy an ice-cream cone and eat it in the bright sunshine of a summer afternoon. She wanted something better than what Heart Mountain could offer.

And it was not only for her son that my grandmother was anxious. She began to resent the sameness in all the faces, the dark hair and eyes, and even more so, in all the thinking. "*Shikataganai*," everybody would say with a shrug of their shoulders. *You cannot change the conditions of your life, so just accept them.* She grew fed up with this pervasive apathy that seemed to infect everyone, the depression, the looks on people's faces that announced they'd given up.

And yet, my grandmother had not resisted or complained either. She, too, was stuck in a pit of indifference, and she knew it. There were those who protested their subjugation, those infamous No-No Boys, who answered "no" to two important questions on their loyalty questionnaires, plus other "troublemakers" who were sent to Tule Lake, or federal prison. And in January of 1944, when Secretary of War Henry L. Stimson had ruled that Japanese Americans were eligible for the draft, some young men rebelled by refusing to serve in the armed forces of a government that imprisoned them and their families. In fact, sixty-three Heart Mountain men were convicted and sentenced by a Wyoming judge to three years in a federal penitentiary for draft resistance. As a person who had been raised with an emphasis on obeying the rules, though, my grandmother never would have opposed the U.S. government, at least not openly. Doing so would have felt like a direct defiance to Mama and Papa, like she was turning her back on everything they stood for. Of course, she was probably frightened, too. She could not afford to be sent away, away from Charles, Ojichan, Papa, and Mama, even out of principle.

And so as 1944 passed slowly, once again Obaachan absorbed herself in novels, hauling my infant uncle to the library, exchanging one book for another. As the September snow began to fall and the boy's feeding schedule stretched to every three hours, she found that she could almost enjoy the stillness of afternoons in her small room. Ojichan stoked the coal stove in the mornings before he left for work, and after Charles had fallen asleep, she would pull her cot toward the stove, bury herself beneath the army-issued wool blanket, and read. In books, she could enjoy the illusion of being someone else, in another time, another country, another world. She was not in Wyoming, trapped by long lines of fence and surrounded by an endless brown expanse. Instead, she was Jane Eyre coming back to find Mr. Rochester, pitying his blindness and loving him more than before.

She was Elizabeth Bennet, discovering the true nature of the elusive Mr. Darcy. She was anyone but herself.

But changes, my grandmother would soon realize, could come as unexpectedly as a Wyoming storm. One moment, not a cloud could be seen in the sky; the next moment, ominous thunder echoed across the plains. One moment, she was chatting with friends on the front steps of her family's church; the next moment, Japan bombed Pearl Harbor and threw the world into a frenzy. One moment, she was in despair about spending her life at Heart Mountain; the next moment, she and Ojichan were hastily making arrangements to leave.

It was a chilly afternoon in the fall of 1944 when my grandfather arrived at their room in Block 17, breathless, full of excitement. There was a posting, he explained to Obaachan, on the bulletin board at the community center. There were job openings for young, able-bodied people willing to leave Heart Mountain. "A man has a factory, a farm and factory, actually, and he's willing to relocate people from the camps to come and work for him. He'll provide housing, plus we'll be paid." Most importantly, the three of them could leave Heart Mountain, its short but stifling summers; its white, tiring winters; the lack of privacy; the rumors and gossip. He would not have had to explain all of this to my grandmother. She knew this was an opportunity to leave and finally have a chance to live their lives on their own terms.

Obaachan was of course interested, and Ojichan immediately began to investigate the details of the factory. When my grandmother tells me this story, I sense that she and my grandfather saw the possibility of moving, and starting from scratch, as a simple decision, something they did not have to ponder too much, and certainly not something to be viewed with any suspicion. And yet my own instinct is to question the motives of the factory owner, Mr. Charles F. Seabrook. Clearly, he had much to gain in offering a way out of prison—the only way out, really, at that time—to young Japanese Americans like my grandparents. How trusting they must have been, how desperate to take on any risk, if that risk would allow them to get out of Heart Mountain. But what life lay ahead for them? Might it be worse, more demanding, more crowded, more suffocating, than their square-mile existence in Wyoming? Was Mr. Seabrook an honest man, or might he cheat them, as the minister had done with the rent money? And what about Obaachan's parents? What about Mama? I'm sure these questions might have crossed my grandparents' minds, but the desire to leave and start over must have overpowered their doubts and concerns.

"What's the name of the place again?" Obaachan's Papa asked my grandfather, taking a puff on the cigarette he had just rolled. He tapped it lightly on the edge of the porch steps, letting the ashes fall to the dry dirt and the crust of old snow.

"Seabrook Farms. They grow and package frozen foods," Ojichan told him in Japanese. "From what I understand, it's a pretty big operation." I imagine my grandfather would've tried his best to sound confident in this conversation—he would've wanted to sound like he knew what he was doing when he explained his plans to move to Obaachan's father. Of course, there was no way he could really know what type of life awaited them on the other side of the country, and my great-grandfather was aware of that. Plus, my grandfather, with his knack for storytelling, might have taken the liberty of filling in any missing details.

"And where is it located?"

"New Jersey. It's far, I know, all the way on the East Coast. But they provide housing, and there will be a job for me."

Obaachan's Papa said nothing for a moment, but his shoulders sagged a little bit as he looked off toward the mountain, high above the plain, the peak white with snow. Watching his daughter, son-in-law, and new grandson leave would be difficult, but he had never been one to meddle in his children's affairs, especially after they were married. When his oldest child, Obaachan's sister, Sachiko, had announced that she would be going to prison with her husband's family, not hers, Papa hadn't uttered a word of protest. Despite any worries he might have had, Papa knew, as my grandparents did, that an opportunity to leave and start a free life might not come again for some time—if ever. He sighed and took another puff. "This is a good opportunity for you. It's a chance to get out of here, to really start life together."

By the fall of 1944, the tide of the war had clearly turned in favor of the Allies, and my family would have at least had some reason to hope that it might end soon. In Europe, on June 6, over 160,000 Allied troops had landed on the French coastline and had begun fighting on the beaches of Normandy. By August, Paris, occupied for four years by the Germans, had been liberated. In October, Athens was liberated. That same month, General Erwin Rommel, the infamous "Desert Fox," who had tormented the British in Northern Africa, committed suicide.

The Allies found success in the Pacific theatre as well. American forces won the island of Saipan, strategically important to both the Allies and the Japanese, in the Battle of the Philippine Sea. A vicious and bloody battle, this loss was especially terrible for Japan, with only one thousand of their thirty thousand troops surviving it. Especially shocking for American troops invading Saipan, however, was the large number of Japanese civilians who, petrified of capture and ill treatment at the hands of American troops (a result of vehement propaganda on the part of the Japanese government), committed suicide. After this event, the Japanese government began encouraging all its citizens to follow suit. Military policy had always been death before surrender—but after the loss at Saipan, it became civilian policy, too.

Still, despite the possibility of the war ending sometime in the near future, my grandparents decided to take the opportunity to leave Heart Mountain. And so, quite suddenly, the two of them were packing up the few belongings they had accumulated during their nearly three-year stay at Heart Mountain—the herringbone suit Obaachan had worn on her wedding day, the calico maternity smocks she had sewn, the crocheted baby blanket from the Philadelphia Quakers, the barely used ice skates ordered from the Montgomery Ward catalog, my grandfather's tall leather boots, and a handful of other items—and preparing to leave their small room in Block 17.

Their departure, I imagine, must have brought a strange blend of emotions. On one hand, they would have been elated to leave. My grandmother would have looked forward to escaping that *shikataganai* attitude that saturated the camp. At the same time, she must have understood that leaving would also involve saying goodbye to Mama, whose health had steadily

deteriorated since their arrival. She would've understood that she was risking not seeing her mother again.
And she must have feared the unknown. While their life
at Heart Mountain was undesirable, at least they knew
what to expect. In New Jersey, they would not have the
support of family and friends. There, for the first time,
Obaachan and Ojichan would really be alone.

On their final morning in Block 17, Obaachan
swept the dust out of the small apartment with the
worn yellow broom she had used every day for over
two years. Their suitcases and bundles were already
outside. Ojichan stood in the corner watching, holding
Charles. Mama, by this point too weak to get out of
bed, remained in her room across the street. Solemnly,
my grandparents said their goodbyes to Obaachan's
parents. They loaded their belongings onto the bus,
and drove off.

The bus took them—there were about twenty
people in all, mostly younger folks like my grandparents—to Billings, Montana. There, my grandmother
recalls going to a restaurant for dinner and ordering a
steak. Ojichan insisted on some small gesture of celebration. It would have been the first time in years that they
could actually choose what to eat, rather than eating
what the servers in the mess hall piled on their plates. It
would have been the first time my grandparents shared
a meal together at a restaurant as well. Without a doubt,

however, there would have been some stares from the *hakujin* folks who lived in Billings. While Montanans might have been accustomed to seeing work crews of Japanese prisoners in the sugar-beet fields, they would not have felt too comfortable seeing them walking their streets or eating at their tables.

After a night in Billings, my grandparents caught a train to Chicago, where they stayed overnight in a hostel that was run by Japanese people. (Only those Japanese living on the West Coast had been evacuated; those who lived inland or on the East Coast were not sent to prison camps during the war. Still, although they were permitted to stay in their homes, I imagine they faced their own struggles outside the barbed wire.) The next morning, my grandparents took another train to Philadelphia, where a bus from Seabrook Farms was waiting for them. As they boarded that bus in Pennsylvania, and as Obaachan observed the anxious faces of the few other families who had come with them on their long journey, the reality sank in: Heart Mountain was now two thousand miles behind them.

On my parents' back porch, my father finishes the last sip of his beer, folds over the corner of a page to mark his reading spot, and stands up. He checks the white bucket hanging from the pergola and fingers the skinny tomato plant hanging upside down from it. He shakes his head.

"People at work say this is the best way to grow tomatoes," he says. "I thought I'd give it a try, but as you can see, it's not very impressive." His other tomatoes, planted in his garden, are staked to support the bulging red fruit. The bucket tomato has not even blossomed.

He needs to pick the Hungarian Wax in the garden, he tells me. As usual, there are hundreds of those hot yellow peppers, and they'll need to be pickled and canned or stuffed with meat and frozen because there are too many to eat fresh. "Mom's going to have her hands full." He squeezes my shoulder as he walks past. "Things will work out with your Obaachan," he says. "It's not your place to worry about it."

Chapter 14

A FEW WEEKS AFTER I LEARN ABOUT THE FAMILY'S PLANS to relocate Obaachan, my mother decides to attend her fortieth high school reunion—her first ever—and she asks if I would like to join her on her trip back to South Jersey, to the small village near Seabrook Farms where she grew up. "There's a museum in Seabrook," she says, hoping to convince me to make the five-hour trek with her. "It has information about the factory where Obaachan and Ojichan both worked. Photos and other things that people have donated. Maybe even some artifacts. Plus you can see where all of us lived. The house, and where I went to school, and where your grandparents were after they left Heart Mountain."

Since I've never been to my mother's hometown, the place where my grandparents began life after their years in a Wyoming concentration camp, I can't resist the opportunity. I agree to go along. On Black Friday, the two of us are crossing the eastern half of the state, driving through swarms of traffic in Harrisburg and Lancaster. (I insist we avoid Philadelphia and instead we veer south through Delaware and must cross a long bridge over the Chesapeake. As we cross it, however, that inherited fear of bridges takes hold, and I regret my decision.) I grip the wheel, knuckles white, palms clammy.

"South Jersey is very pretty," my mother tells me as we drive, looking straight ahead. "You know New Jersey is called the Garden State, don't you? It's all farms."

I remind her that things might be different, that life might have changed in the last forty years, and that she shouldn't expect everything to be as it was when she left. Since I've recently been to northern New Jersey, I have a suspicion that my mother's expectations may be off. She doesn't believe me, though, and feels sure that her beloved Garden State will be little changed since the fifties.

After four hours of driving, at last we cross into New Jersey. Immediately, I'm struck by the long, wide fields, the endless rows of soybeans, the giant irrigation systems stretching across the countryside, the absence of highways. "See," my mother says, looking out the window, taking in the farms that have not altered in decades.

I have one distinct memory from my grandparents' life in New Jersey, and the memory is not from Seabrook, but from Ocean City, where they initially moved after retiring. In their small condo in Ocean City, Obaachan, Ojichan, my mom, brother, and I cluster at the kitchen table, watching President Reagan on their small, jittery television. I remember that their condominium complex was dark brown on the outside, and that we could walk to the beach, but I don't remember being at the beach or what anything looked like inside their home. I'm not even sure how many times I was there, although I do remember traveling a good bit as a girl, and there are plenty of photographs capturing moments from this era. My mother hauled us kids all over the place back then. My father, who worked various shifts at the time, rarely went along, but Mom was always determined to see her family and therefore made it happen. She didn't believe in eating fast food, and still doesn't, so instead she packed loads of snacks—almonds, raisins, apples, crackers, yogurt—and tucked us into her old mauve Volkswagen Rabbit. She sang songs and had a policy that she would stop at as many ice-cream parlors along the way as we wanted. I could never eat more than one cone of soft serve, so the little green Dairy-Freez along 522 in Orbisonia, about forty-five minutes from our home, was the only place I ever got my ice cream. My mother and brother always tapped out after two. Still, to us children, the sheer idea of unlimited ice cream was thrilling.

Later, when my grandparents moved to Florida, she would drive us there as well, right after school ended, in June, for our annual two-week visit. (I suspect my mother decided to drive, instead of fly, to save money. Even today, when she doesn't really need to worry about money, she only buys things on sale and will travel across town to save a few cents on gas.) On our trips to Florida, we tried to make it to Rocky Mount, North Carolina, on the first day, and then we finished the trip to Melbourne on the second day. "Look through the AAA book for me, honey," my mother would say, "and find the page where they list hotels in Rocky Mount." I was in middle school then, and had recently learned how to read maps in Mr. Cousins's social studies class. Even more than the maps, though, I enjoyed finding the page and making my recommendations about hotels. I was always sure to give her the phone numbers of the places with swimming pools first, knowing how hot the June weather in North Carolina was. On one of our gas stops, my mom would use a pay phone. My brother and I didn't mind the trip too much because we always stopped at the outlet mall in North Carolina, where we could pick out a new pair of Nikes, plus we were permitted to play Nintendo GameBoy in the car. (At home, the GameBoy was always hidden somewhere, and we were not allowed to play with it—my parents disapproved of sedentary childhoods—so its annual appearance was a treat.)

I recall, though, that my mother grew nervous sometimes in the South, especially in those sleepy little towns deep in Georgia, where the drawls were thick and heavy, and where the locals would sit in front of the gas stations, watching as my mother pumped gas. "Lock the doors," she whispered through the crack in the window when she went in to pay for the fuel. I sensed her unease, and it made me uneasy. By that age, maybe eleven or twelve, I'd witnessed my mother's fiery temper and intrepid behavior enough to believe that she was almost fearless. So what was it that made her afraid? "Things still happen to people down here," she said when I asked. "We're not *hakujin*."

In school I'd learned about the Civil War, Lincoln, slavery, Jim Crow, cross burnings, lynchings. (In my Pennsylvania school district, the social studies teachers made sure that we understood that we northerners, benevolent and free of prejudice, were the heroes in that narrative of racism and injustice.) So even though my mother couldn't quite—or perhaps chose not to—articulate her fears that day, I understood what she was getting at.

In New Jersey, at last my mother and I pull into the parking lot of the Seabrook Educational and Cultural

Center, and a man, gray-haired and leaning on a cane, stands at the top of a staircase and watches as I quiet the engine. He runs his hand through his hair and shifts his weight. He's expecting us—my mother made an appointment earlier in the week—and appears to have been waiting.

"Hi," my mother says, stepping out of the car. "Hope we didn't keep you waiting. The traffic was bad through Lancaster."

My mother has already decided that she likes this man's attitude. On the phone, when he introduced himself, he explained that his wife was from the area, but that he was from out of state. He described himself as a "transplant" and not an "outsider." And my mother, having spent most of her adult life as an "outsider" in my father's small town of *hakujin* who never leave the area, likes the distinct difference. "Even after living there for thirty years," she tells me, with a shake of her head, "I'm still not considered a local . . ." She has picked up the habits of the area—hunts whitetail and wild turkey, can cook the Pennsylvania Dutch meals my father's mother has taught her, and even sometimes, accidentally, speaks with that unusual accent that only central Pennsylvanians have—but she is not one of them, and she knows it.

The Seabrook Educational and Cultural Center is located in the basement of the Upper Deerfield

Township building. Our guide is giving us a walking tour of the place, pointing to the photographs of workers in assembly lines and the bright boxes of Seabrook Farms frozen green beans, peas, winter squash, and spinach. He seems frustrated that my mother, having broken off to explore the museum on her own, is not paying attention. He did, after all, extend his Friday hours after much prodding on her part, and he clearly enjoys giving the tours. But all the photographs—the children my mother might have known and places she played and classrooms she studied in—they're too much of a distraction. She examines the pictures of male workers, most of whom are Japanese, looking for images of her father, and she finds one. My Ojichan, then straight backed, wearing a pair of glasses and a white labcoat, is holding a beaker and looks like a scientist. For a few years at Seabrook, he worked in a department that did product research, a position he felt proud of. After showing me the photograph of Ojichan, my mother moves on to studying the class photographs, squinting, reading the dates etched in the corners, hoping to see her brother or sister among the faces.

Seabrook Farms, founded by Charles F. Seabrook (or C. F., as friends and family knew him), opened in 1911. Seabrook, an engineer, devoted a lot of energy to developing irrigation systems and power plants, and before long, Seabrook Farms became a large-scale operation.

The company faced a labor shortage even before the war. When it began supplying the American military with vegetables during the war, however, that shortage became a real concern. The son of C. F., Jack, who was in charge of labor issues at the time, approached the War Relocation Authority and requested the release of Japanese Americans who were willing to move to New Jersey in January of 1944. Within a year of Jack Seabrook's request, Obaachan and Ojichan arrived at Seabrook Farms, ready to work.

"Now, which camps were your grandparents at?" the guide asks me, glancing at my mother with a look of disapproval as she continues to lag farther and farther behind. I tell him they lived at Heart Mountain, Wyoming, but that both were originally from California.

"So they would've gotten here fall of '44?" he asks, his brows furrowed, his mind shuffling through the dates. I tell him that's correct. "There were a few from Heart Mountain, around twenty-five hundred. But we had people all the way from South America," he continues. "A woman who volunteers here, a Japanese woman, she came all the way from Peru."

After the bombing of Pearl Harbor, the United States began pressuring other countries in the West to round up their Japanese. Canada, already at war with Germany and Italy, declared war on Japan within hours of the attack on December 7, 1941, and after learning of the United States' plans to relocate its Japanese in the early months of 1942, it quickly followed suit. Over twenty-one thousand Japanese Canadians, most of whom resided in British Columbia, were sent to the nation's interior, where they lived out the duration of the war in abandoned mining towns, sugar-beet farms, lumber camps, and road-construction camps. They were not permitted to return to British Columbia until 1949, long after the war was over.

Many Latin American countries also complied with the United States, which cited the safety of the Panama Canal as its reason for requesting the deportation of Japanese. Peru, although not involved in the war, turned over around a thousand people of Japanese ancestry to American authorities. Cuba incarcerated all adult male Japanese. Although Brazil, Chile, and Argentina did not get involved in the roundup, overall, 2,264 Japanese were sent to the United States from Latin America and the Caribbean. In April of 1942, the transfers began, with many Japanese being sent to Crystal City, Texas. But not all of the Latin American Japanese were so lucky as to spend the war in a family facility in Texas. Nearly three thousand boarded the Swedish ship *Gripsholm* and were exchanged for American citizens who'd been captured in the Pacific. In fact, almost half of the Japanese prisoners exchanged during the war were from Latin America, not the United States.

At Seabrook Farms, it was not only evacuees of Japanese descent like my grandparents who put down roots and tried to raise families. Although they made up the majority of the population, other workers were also recruited by Seabrook Farms. With the war raging on, the prospect of employment and housing appealed to many, regardless of their race. Latvians, Italians, Germans, African Americans, and many others came to work at Seabrook Farms, all of them trying to start a new life, all of them starting from scratch. Some were war refugees; some came from the deep South. There were even German POWs who worked there. Although many of the employees barely spoke English, they managed to be friendly to each other, despite all their differences.

My mother remembers loving the ethnic diversity of this place. "My friend's German mother always made the most wonderful chocolate cake," she recalls. "And my classes, they were full of people from all over. It was a wonderful place to grow up."

Her fond memories of Seabrook, however, were preceded by difficult years for my grandparents. Like the other workers at Seabrook Farms, Ojichan worked twelve-hour days, with one day off every two weeks, and he earned between thirty-five and fifty cents an hour. The fact that my grandparents had a toddler at the time wouldn't have helped matters either, I'm sure.

But the three of them had a brand-new apartment, and all the utilities were paid.

Obaachan, having never cooked on a brand-new stove or lived in a place with such sparkling white walls, even in the house on Pico Street back in Los Angeles, viewed their apartment with some excitement. Although it was a simple concrete-block building that was not any more luxurious than their home at Heart Mountain, she took great care in keeping it clean and tidy. My grandfather wouldn't have had it otherwise. She relished the space and savored the meals at a normal kitchen table, rather than at a mess hall.

"We were so poor," Obaachan told me once, shaking her head, wrinkling her nose. "I think we ate baked beans and carrot sticks almost every meal. A little protein, plus a vegetable. Those were the cheapest things I could get." The truth was, they had eaten better food at Heart Mountain—at least there, sometimes they had meat—but my grandmother still insists they had no regrets about leaving, despite struggling to piece together these meager meals.

For the first time since they'd met, my grandparents were free to come and go as they pleased. No armed guards eyed them suspiciously, no chaperones had to accompany them if they needed to go somewhere, and no identification passes had to be carried. In contrast to their life in camp, it seemed that every day brought with it a fresh hope of what the future might hold. The spring after their arrival, my grandmother bought a stroller for Charles. They saved up and were finally able to afford one. In the afternoons, she would take my young uncle for a walk around Seabrook, showing him the children playing in their yards, pausing to admire the daffodils.

It was nine months after my grandparents left Wyoming when a telegram from Obaachan's Papa arrived, on a sultry day in August 1945. According to the newspapers, which my grandparents tried to read regularly, the war was very close to ending. Germany had surrendered that spring, on May 7. The Allies had dropped atomic bombs on the cities of Hiroshima on August 6, and on Nagasaki on August 9. Peace, it seemed, might finally be within reach.

Obaachan was scrubbing the kitchen floor, her hands submerged in a bucket of steaming water and ammonia, wringing out a rag from an old shirt. Ojichan was at work, and little Charles was napping. When she heard the knock on the door and looked out to see the deliveryman in his starched blue uniform standing on the step, she felt a sharp tug at her chest, and she could barely cough out a thank you when she took the piece of paper into her hand. Without opening it, she knew what it said, and feared it. And despite the years of warnings from the doctors, the fact that she herself had witnessed the deterioration, the pain of the news was still piercing: her mother was dead.

One of the more famous photographs from World War II is that of an American sailor in Time Square, kissing a young woman, her back arched, the soldier holding her tight. In the background, intense celebration occurs. Taken on August 14, 1945, and originally published in *Life* magazine, the photograph was taken on V-J Day, the day the American people learned of Japan's surrender. At last, nearly four years after Japan had bombed Pearl Harbor, the war was over.

During those years, over 16 million Americans had served in the armed forces. Of those, 671,000 had been wounded, and 405,399 had given their lives. For a country that had, like the rest of the world, witnessed terrible atrocities, experienced devastating and abundant losses during the war, and learned, firsthand, just how cruel human beings could be to one another, news of Japan's surrender was more than just news that the war had ended. It signaled possibilities—that people could begin resurrecting their families, homes, and lives from the rubble. Of course, my grandparents, and the 120,000 other Japanese Americans who'd spent the war in prison, would have welcomed this news just as much as other Americans. For them, it meant that they would not have to spend the rest of their lives behind barbed wire.

In a strange twist of fate, though—or maybe just a stroke of bad luck—it was on this day of great celebration in the United States that my grandmother had to begin the long trip back to Heart Mountain to bury her mother. She and Ojichan could barely scrape up enough money to purchase one train ticket, to say nothing of two, so they'd decided that Obaachan would go alone, while my grandfather stayed in Seabrook and looked after Charles. Although Obaachan hated to part with Charles, toting an infant all the way to Wyoming and then having him there at the funeral would have made an already-difficult trip more difficult, especially since Ojichan would not be along to help.

"I'll see you in a week," Ojichan whispered to my grandmother, holding her close. In that intimate moment, my grandfather must have remembered losing his father, who died of *gan*, or cancer, shortly after Ojichan had left Japan. My grandfather had never really had a chance to say goodbye. Obaachan knelt and pulled Charles from his stroller, holding him to her chest. Unable to clear the knot in her throat, she struggled to speak. She nodded, turned away, and boarded the train. Before her was a long, frightening journey.

"This was the only time I was really, really afraid," Obaachan has admitted, her eyes wide and eyebrows raised. Of all the upsetting moments she had experienced—the hysteria that pervaded the West Coast after the bombing of Pearl Harbor, the bus ride to Pomona through swarms of angry people, the long train ride from California to Heart Mountain—that trip from Seabrook Farms to Wyoming was the worst. My grandmother, always easily intimidated, was the only nonwhite on the train that day. Most of the passengers were sailors, who walked up and down the aisles of the train shaking people's hands, congratulating each other, and enjoying the momentous occasion.

Obaachan watched out the window, sinking low in her seat, hoping to remain inconspicuous, with her tiny frame and very small suitcase. Out of respect for her mother, she wore black. As the train heaved its way across Pennsylvania, and then Ohio, and all those other states that separated her new life in New Jersey from that existence in Wyoming, she simply looked out the window, watching the landscape drift past, praying.

I can't help wondering if perhaps on that August day, my grandmother regretted her decision to leave Heart Mountain to move to New Jersey. Did her fear cause her to doubt herself? Did she feel that she should have been there for her mother in those final months? Obaachan's emotions were no doubt complicated by the mood of the train on that August afternoon, and by the fact that she had left her husband and son behind. But returning to Heart Mountain must have been difficult as well. To this day my grandmother has no desire to go back. Once, I asked her if she would ever want to return, just to see things, and she turned to me with a blended look of disbelief and disgust. I was crazy to ask such a question, she seemed to say. "No, of course not," she told me firmly. "I will never go back. Never."

Obaachan has photographs of her mother's funeral at Heart Mountain: a large group of mourners dressed in black, lined up around a large casket adorned with two wreaths. My grandmother stands in the front row of the photograph, her head hung so low that her face is completely invisible. If she had not pointed herself out to me, I would not have known it was her.

Within three months of my great-grandmother's funeral, by November 10, 1945, every prisoner at Heart Mountain was gone. In fact, all the camps closed shortly after V-J Day. The prisoners were given $25 cash and told to make arrangements for themselves. Obaachan's sister, my great-aunt, who'd spent the war in a camp in Arkansas, returned to California with her husband and child. My great uncles, Obaachan's brothers, who'd served in the military and had never been interned, eventually went back to California as well. Papa, with all of his children grown and with his wife gone, moved to New York City with his brother Kisho, the one who'd owned the successful Chinese restaurant back in Los Angeles. Together, the two of them opened and ran a small hotel near Columbia University. Though he and my grandparents did not live all that far away from each other—he in New York and they in New Jersey—after the war ended, they didn't see one another very frequently. Papa passed away in the 1960s. He never remarried. He never gardened again either.

When our tour of the Seabrook Educational and Cultural Center has ended, the director takes a picture of my mother and me, and informs us that he'll add it to the bulletin board of other visitors. He leans on his cane and thanks us for coming, points us to a rack of books and other knickknacks for sale. My mother buys four matching purple T-shirts that say Seabrook, one for herself and one for each of her siblings.

"I'd like to drive around," she says as we exit the building, buttoning her jacket against the cool afternoon, "past my old house and the elementary school. I'd like you to take some pictures."

We climb into the car and drive out of the parking lot, and I follow my mother's directions: turn left here, pull in right there. I photograph her standing in front of her old school, near the tall steps that stretch all the way up to the front door. Next, we head to the street where she grew up. Even though a new family now lives in their old house, she insists on a photograph of herself in front of it. Reluctantly, I turn off the ignition and crawl out of the car again.

"People live here," I say quietly, as if the new owners might hear me from inside. There are cars parked in the driveway. "You can't just stand in someone's yard." Having grown up in central Pennsylvania, where landowners post their acreage with black-and-orange signs and take the crime of trespassing seriously, I've always been mindful of encroaching on other people's property.

"If they come out, I'll just tell them this is where I grew up," my mother says. In this moment, her sense that any misunderstanding could be easily handled with a conversation reminds me of my grandfather. Like him, she's not at all shy, and she is always happy to talk to anyone. She jogs over to the mailbox and stands in the lawn, grinning, thrilled. I feel guilty for tainting the experience with my warnings and embarrassment.

The house, a small yellow ranch, has fallen into mild disrepair, with the windows old, the screens dirty, and the siding dull and discolored. The lawn is overgrown, and weeds grow from the cracks in the sidewalk. This is where my grandparents moved after they lived in the concrete-block apartment. My mother, the third child and born in 1948, never lived at that first place.

"Did you get it?" she asks, still smiling for the camera. I tell her I took two pictures and show her the images on the small camera screen. "Good," she says. We drive around Seabrook and the neighboring towns, stopping twice for subs, once at a small one-story building that looks like it might have been a gas station fifty years ago, and also at a quaint shop with wide wooden-plank flooring. My mother says the subs in South Jersey are the best in the world, and she intends to get her fill since she hasn't been here for so long. She sits in the passenger seat, her fingers wet with olive oil, watching out the window and eating. At her age, my mother can still outeat me, and yet she manages to stay thin. (I'm convinced this is because she rarely sits in one place for more than ten minutes.)

For the reunion, held at a local country club, my mother has borrowed from a friend a black dress, knee length and with a few discreet gemstones near the neck. She curls her hair and slips on a pair of heels. "Everyone will be jealous," I tell her as she prepares to leave the hotel.

The rest of our weekend in New Jersey consists of taking a few more snapshots of favorite places, and after we've made all the stops on my mother's itinerary, we head back, across the wide Chesapeake again, through the midsection of Pennsylvania, home.

Chapter 15

ITEM BY ITEM, OBAACHAN IS PACKING UP HER HOUSE IN
Florida. My family has decided that it makes most sense
for her to move to Pennsylvania, to live near my mother,
who the siblings agree is the best caregiver of the four
of them. Relocating my grandmother to Pennsylvania
means that she'll live closer to me as well, so I suppose I
should be happy about it. In a few weeks, she will drive
up the coast in a U-Haul with my uncle Jay, with what's
left of her belongings on board.

When I arrive for what we both know will be my
final visit to her place in Florida, I'm struck immediately by the sparseness inside. The painting of a swamp
that used to hang above the couch in the living room,
with its tans, yellows, and grays, is gone. The collection
of family photographs on the spare-room bookshelf—
weddings, school pictures from grandchildren, family

vacations—has been packed up. The Japanese doll, posed in a long navy *kimono*, that used to sit on the glass table near the entryway, has been removed. About half of Obaachan's furniture isn't there either.

"The Salvation Army has already been here once," she tells me as we walk into the living room. "They took the one bed, and later, I'll give them the glass table where I do my Sudoku puzzles and one of the couches. But the other has a tear in the back, so they won't take it." The Salvation Army refuses any furniture that's damaged, she explains, then looks at me with a grin. "Maybe I can sell it on craigslist." My uncle, who has gotten rid of lots of unwanted items through this website, including a free artificial Christmas tree that thirty people wanted, has told her about the wonders of craigslist. Obaachan insists she has no interest in using the Internet, but she still likes to "know what's going on" in the world of cyberspace.

"All of this packing, it's kind of like at Heart Mountain," Obaachan says, gesturing toward the walls and empty space of her kitchen. Just as she would have done sixty years earlier, my grandmother must evaluate, piece by piece, what she truly wishes to take with her. Obaachan looks at me, searches my face for a brief moment. "I packed up everything except for two plates, two bowls, two sets of silverware, two glasses. Plus one pot and one frying pan." She shrugs. "You'd be surprised at how little you really need. You learn to be resourceful."

She uses the stainless-steel pot to cook her oatmeal in the mornings and to steam brown rice. She can simmer soups and make popcorn in that pot as well. In the frying pan, she can cook an egg for *sukiyaki* or sauté some fresh vegetables for stir-fry. Determined to use up the items in her pantry rather than throw them away or haul them to Pennsylvania, she has grown creative in her cooking.

"Your uncle wants to have the grapefruit trees cut down," Obaachan tells me as she peers out the kitchen window, frowning. "He's thinking about resale, you know. He says they're ugly." The grapefruit trees are not as graceful as they once were, a few years ago, when I'd climb the trunk and shimmy across the limbs, plucking fruit and dropping it into a cardboard box. With each of the more violent storms that have begun hitting central Florida, the trees have grown a little more worn, a little less green. But they still bear fruit. Plus, my grandparents planted them together when they first moved here, two small plants, and in twenty-one years, they have grown full-size. Ojichan, I feel sure, would have disapproved of this plan to remove the trees and would have put up a fight about it. But Obaachan won't say a word. I suspect that in her mind, she feels she should be grateful for the twenty plus years of rent-free living she enjoyed here. Besides, it's not in her nature to argue about these types of things.

"I found something of Ojichan's," she tells me later that evening. She shuffles into the spare room where I am reading, hands me a worn leather-bound rectangular photo album, about six-by-twelve inches, and sits down at her wicker-and-glass table set. "It's some pictures and some things that he wrote. Back when I first found it, a number of years ago, I had to get my sister to translate it because it's in Japanese. So all the notes in English, they're hers." Although Obaachan grew up speaking Japanese with her friends and family in Los Angeles, she and my grandfather never spoke the language at home and chose not to teach their children. After the war, they no doubt thought it best to avoid practices that might lead neighbors to believe they weren't "American." Today, after decades of not speaking Japanese, my grandmother barely remembers the language of her youth.

I open the album, run my fingers gently over the black pages. My grandfather has written in white ink in the margins. The translated notes, all on different scraps of paper, are in the handwriting of the great-aunt I've never met. I leaf through the album. A black-and-white photograph of the long bridge with its series of arches, stretching over a wide river. A beautiful picture of a grove of cherry trees, in full blossom, with two groups of people seated beneath them, dated 1934. My grandfather's Japanese characters—the language he tried to teach me at the kitchen table when I was young— stretch vertically beside the photograph. Ojichan would have crossed this bridge each morning on his way to school.

A piece of paper from my great-aunt slides out. I squint at her translation. Most of Ojichan's notes are done in a sort of poetry, she writes, so the translating is difficult:

"I think about each tree and have deep memories. Think about singing that song—*o-te te tsunaide*—in my kindergarten days . . . I think about the village of Iwakuni with buds and blossoms appearing in the early spring. The natural sounds of the mountain and the river remind me of dreams of my home country that I left behind."

There are other photographs, too, and more notes. In one picture, a group of men are leaning over, working the earth. San Francisco, August 16, 1938, it says, and in the margin Ojichan has written this: "No matter where you go in the world, people are close to nature and like to mix with the earth. Here they are hoeing, and it reminds me of home, and I feel sad."

Then there are a series of three photographs of my grandfather in America. He is leaning against a car, ankles crossed, hand on hip. The caption reads: "Taken near Star Florist Shop. Feeling very homesick." And beneath that, a lengthier note: "Living alone in a foreign country without parents, siblings, or friends, trying to keep pace with society here, was painful and sad. Without education and personality, being 'driven' in a foreign culture was difficult and painful. It's a wonder that with a constant feeling of agony in my heart, that this little body was able to withstand all the difficulties I faced."

As I read the words of my grandfather in this album, at last I am able to better understand his tragedy. How intense his struggle must have been here in America, a teenager alone in a country of strangers, in the 1930s. Who was there to listen to him? How would he have known whom to trust? His words in the album are marked by a loneliness and lostness that I never saw in him, so many decades later—that he grew out of, or hid, perhaps, even from his wife. Although he never fully lost that tendency toward wildness that brought about his coming to America in the first place, he never mentioned just how deeply he missed his homeland either. He never used the word "regret" when he talked about that dreadful decision to throw a stone at the statue's face, at least not when he spoke to us children about it, but he must have felt some remorse for that action, especially in his early years in this country.

I ask Obaachan if he ever considered returning.

"No, never. My husband never wanted to go back to Japan," Obaachan says, shaking her head for emphasis, "even when he received the telegram from his family saying that his father had *gan*, or cancer, and insisting that he come home right away. When his father got sick, it was not that long after he came to America, but he knew already he would never go back." Later on, after my grandparents were married, they tried to bring Ojichan's mother, by that time a widow, to the United States, but there was a long waiting list for people from Japan—families who'd been separated, for instance—who wanted to come to America after the war. She died before her name was reached.

"Ojichan always said, 'I would be dead by now,'" Obaachan says. She pauses. "That's the way he looked at it. He meant the war."

With over two million combat casualties and an estimated 580,000 civilian deaths, Japan lost nearly four percent of its population during World War II. Many of those combat casualties would have been young men, around my grandfather's age. Ironically, my grandfather's foolish behavior as a teenager—throwing that rock at the statue—and his parents' severe response—sending him to America, alone—may have saved his life.

It would be a stretch, I think, some weak but treacherous attempt to find the enormous ripples of that single action, to unite too many events—my grandparents' marriage, the birth of their children, my own life and my brother's—to the throwing of that stone back in 1938. Doing so would somehow trivialize everything about my own existence. But the idea does flicker through my mind, tempting me, daring me to make that link.

The next morning, in the courtyard of Obaachan's house, the two of us sit at the glass table, finishing our bowls of chicken salsa soup. A light breeze lifts the spindly branches of Obaachan's two tomato plants, which we just planted the day before. Before my grandfather passed away, he made a wheeled platform for potted plants so that he and Obaachan could easily maneuver them around the courtyard. If there's a thunderstorm with high winds, for instance, Obaachan can easily wheel all of her plants closer to the house, where they're protected by the roof's overhang.

"Ever since you started asking me about all of this, the war, Heart Mountain," Obaachan says, folding her napkin and placing it on the table, "I've been trying to think about why this happened to me. I could have died from spinal meningitis when I was eight. Another time, when Papa took me with him to buy *sashimi*, I was almost hit by a car. Two times in my childhood, I came very close to dying. But I didn't. So now I'm asking myself *why*. Why did I live?"

She forms this question carefully, frowning at the way the words feel on her lips, as though the idea has not occurred to her until recently. I ask her if she has come up with an answer, and she frowns, shrugs just a little. "I think maybe I survived because I was supposed to raise my four children, you know, be a good mother," she says slowly. All four of them grew up to be good, hard-working people, and she is proud of them. "I guess I'm still figuring it out," she adds. "But I believe everyone has a purpose," Obaachan continues. "I believe that, and I always have." She pauses again. "The answer will come to me," she says quietly, with confidence, looking out over the garden, at the tall bird-of-paradise arcing at the entrance, at the full, red hibiscus waving in the breeze, vibrant.

Bibliography

Conrat, Maisie & Richard. *Executive Order 9066: The Internment of 110,000 Japanese Americans.* Los Angeles, CA: California Historical Society, 1972.

Daniels, Roger. *Concentration Camps: North America.* Malabar, FL: Robert E. Krieger Publishing Company, Inc., 1981.

—. *Concentration Camps USA: Japanese Americans and World War II.* New York: Holt, Rinehart and Winston, Inc., 1972.

—. *Prisoners without Trial: Japanese Americans in World War II.* Revised ed. New York: Hill and Wang, 2004.

DeWitt, John L. *Final Report: Japanese Evacuation from the West Coast, 1942.* Washington, D.C.: Government Printing Office, 1943.

Fugita, Stephen S. & Fernandez, Marilyn. *Altered Lives, Enduring Community: Japanese Americans Remember Their World War II Incarceration.* Seattle: Washington University Press, 2004.

Hong Kingston, Maxine. "No Name Woman." *The Best American Essays of the Twentieth Century.* Ed. Joyce Carol Oates & Robert Atwan. Boston: Houghton Mifflin Company, 2000.

Ishigo, Estelle. *Lone Heart Mountain*. Los Angeles, CA: Anderson, Ritchie & Simon, 1972.

Kashima, Tetsuden. *Judgment without Trial: Japanese American Imprisonment during World War II*. Seattle: University of Washington Press, 2003.

Komoda, Shusui & Pointner, Horst. *Ikebana: Spirit and Technique*. Dorset, England: Blandford Press, Ltd., 1976.

Lagnado, Lucette. *The Man in the White Sharkskin Suit*. New York: HarperCollins, 2007.

Mackey, Mike. *Heart Mountain: Life in Wyoming's Concentration Camp*. Powell, Wyoming: Western History Publications, 2000.

Meyer, Dillon S. *Uprooted Americans: The Japanese Americans and the War Relocation Authority during World War II*. Tucson: The University of Arizona Press, 1971.

Spicer, Edward H., Hansen, Asael T., Luomala, Katherine, & Opler, Marvin K. *Impounded People: Japanese-Americans in the Relocation Centers*. Tucson: The University of Arizona Press, 1969.

Spiegelman, Art. *Maus I*. New York: Pantheon Books, 1986.

U.S. Department of the Interior. *Wartime Exile: The Exclusion of Japanese Americans from the West Coast*. Washington, D.C.: Government Printing Office.

Wakatski, Jeanne. *Farewell to Manzanar*. New York: Bantam, 1973.

Additional Bibliographic Notes

For a timeline of the internment of the Japanese Americans, along with useful links to the various executive orders related to their internment, I used this site:

http://www.pbs.org/childofcamp/history/timeline.html

I am grateful to independent historian Mike Mackey, who never seemed to tire of my emailed questions about Heart Mountain. His essay "A Brief History of the Heart Mountain Relocation Center and the Japanese American Experience" was especially useful in developing a stronger sense of everyday life at Heart Mountain. It also features some interesting photographs from the camp. It's available at:

http://chem.nwc.cc.wy.us/HMDP/history.htm

All of my information about Pomona before 1942 was found at:

http://www.fairplex.com/fp/AboutUs/History/1920s.asp

I found much of my information on the progress of the war at:

http://www.pbs.org/perilousfight/

For my details on the Battle of Guadalcanal, I used this website:

http://www.guadalcanal.com/battleofguadalcanal.html

All of my information about the deportation of Canadian and Latin American Japanese is from:

http://www.nps.gov/history/history/online_books/anthropology74/ce3m.htm